READING AND BELIEVING

Program in Judaic Studies
Brown University
BROWN JUDAIC STUDIES

Edited by
Jacob Neusner,
Wendell S. Dietrich, Ernest S. Frerichs,
Calvin Goldscheider, Alan Zuckerman

Project Editors (Project)

David Blumenthal, Emory University (Approaches to Medieval Judaism)
William Brinner (Studies in Judaism and Islam)
Ernest S. Frerichs, Brown University (Dissertations and Monographs)
Lenn Evan Goodman, University of Hawaii (Studies in Medieval Judaism) (Studies in
Judaism and Islam)
William Scott Green, University of Rochester (Approaches to Ancient Judaism)
Ivan Marcus, Jewish Theological Seminary of America
(Texts and Studies in Medieval Judaism)
Marc L. Raphael, Ohio State University (Approaches to Judaism in Modern Times)
Norbert Samuelson, Temple University (Jewish Philosophy)
Jonathan Z. Smith, University of Chicago (Studia Philonica)

Number 113
READING AND BELIEVING
Ancient Judaism and
Contemporary Gullibility
by
Jacob Neusner

READING AND BELIEVING
Ancient Judaism and
Contemporary Gullibility

by
Jacob Neusner

Scholars Press
Atlanta, Georgia

READING AND BELIEVING
Ancient Judaism and
Contemporary Gullibility

© 1986
Brown University

Library of Congress Cataloging in Publication Data

Neusner, Jacob, 1932
  Reading and believing

  (Brown Judaic studies ; no. 113)
  Includes index.
  1. Judaism—History—To 70 A.D.—Historiography.
  2. Judaism—History—Talmudic period, 10–425—
Historiography.   I. Title.   II. Series.
BM170.N459   1986   296'.072   86-30399
ISBN 0-89130-976-4 (alk. paper)
ISBN 0-89130-977-2 (pbk. : alk. paper)

Printed in the United States of America
on acid-free paper

You state that I am "nearly unaware of the difficulty involved in distinguishing first century Judaism from the late formulations of rabbinic literature." First century rabbinic Judaism is the teachings of the rabbis who lived during that period, and these teachings are recorded faithfully in the Mishnah, Tosefta, and two Talmuds. Are you trying to say that the later rabbis erred, and gave teachings of Bet [the House of] Hillel and Bet [the House of] Shammai, for example, which were not really taught by these Schools? Even Reform and Conservative rabbis who do not accept the authority of these rabbis seldom raise questions on the authenticity of these sources. But even if there be some who do raise such doubts, you are surely aware that most Jews, throughout Jewish history as well as nowadays, do not question the authenticity of these sources. Why should they be questioned any more than statements of Abraham in the Five Books of Moses, or Jesus in the Gospels? Did the ancients seek to delude us? The Karaites, who rejected the Oral Tradition, as well as the Sadducees who believed likewise in Jesus' time, have disappeared long ago from the Jewish scene. It is therefore not principle that is involved. We should either reject everything handed down from the ancients or accept that which has come down from reliable sources.

Letter received by
a New Testament scholar from
a scholar of first-century Judaism.

For

RICHARD EKMAN

My friend and
sometime co-worker
at the National Endowment
For the Humanities

Who
brought about reform
and made no enemies

A worker of
miracles

CONTENTS

Part Three
THE OLD GULLIBILITY REDIVIVUS

Part Four
THE WAY FORWARD

Preface

Judaism now endures in a free society. The intellectual life of Judaism therefore finds itself in an unprecedented situation. Entry of Judaic Studies into the academy marks only one measure of the new circumstance, but makes acute, not merely chronic, the crisis of freedom confronting the received tradition of learning in Judaism. This book is about scholars who have not yet taken up the challenges of freedom to the intellect, in the academy in particular: the public, shared, reasoned, even civil discourse about what was formerly private and parochial to the Jews. They commit one simple error. They ignore the canons of criticism that govern academic scholarship. They take for granted that pretty much everything they read is true -- except what they decide is not true. They cannot and ordinarily do not raise the question of whether an authorship knows what it is talking about, and they do not address the issue of the purpose of a text: historical or imaginative, for example. For them the issue always is history, namely, what really happened, and that issue was settled, so to speak, at Sinai: it is all true (except, on an episodic basis, what is not true, which the scholars somehow know instinctively).

In fact, in my view they all remain well within the walls of the old intellectual ghetto. They exhibit the credulity characteristic of the traditional settings of Judaic studies, Yeshivot and Jewish universities and seminaries in the diaspora and in the State of Israel, and they take not only as fact but at face value everything in the holy books. "Judaism" is special and need not undergo description, analysis, and interpretation in accord with a shared and public canon of rules of criticism. "We all know" how to do the work, and "we" do not have to explain to "outsiders" either what the work is or why it is important. It is a self-evidently important enterprise in the rehearsal of information. Knowing these things the way "we" know them explains the value of knowing these things. That is the mentality of a ghetto, a closed circle, and some Jewish scholars of Judaism in late antiquity have not left the ghetto, nor do they even admit to themselves that they presently reside therein. The simple argument of this book, therefore, is that the old order endures, not everywhere to be sure, but in places in which it otherwise does not belong, specifically, in the academy in the West. In reference to specific statements, cited below, I raise the charge of gullibility, and I plan in this book to make that charge stick. Why gullibility?

People who are gullible generically believe everything they hear, and gullibility as generic generates belief in whatever the holy books say. If, therefore, a canonical ("holy") book says a holy man said something, he really said it, and if the book says he did something, he really did it. That is gullibility. Scholarship in the service of gullibility frames questions that implicitly affirm the accuracy of the holy books, asking questions, for example, that can only be answered in the assumption that the inerrant Scriptures contain the answers -- therefore, as a matter of process, do not err. By extension holy books that tell stories produce history through the paraphrase of stories into historical language: this is what happened, this is how it happened, and here are the reasons why it happened. Scholarship of a credulous character need not serve God, it may serve Satan. Lives of Jesus may portray him as son of God or as magician. Both statements are equally fundamentalist in scholarly premise, the one white, the other black gullibility, the one positive, the other negative. There is no methodological or epistemological difference. Here I demonstrate, only through a careful reading of *ipsissima verba*, that gullibility characterizes nearly all work on ancient Judaism.

The gullibility of which I speak, moreover, characterizes not solely Orthodox believers, from whom one can ask no better, but, deplorably, Conservative, Reform, and national-secular Israeli scholars, who claim to be "critical" and who probably believe they are, as well as among non-Jewish scholars, in the New Testament in particular, who approach the same sources for their own purposes. (But the principal focus of discourse here is on Jewish scholars of ancient Judaism.) I therefore shall show a perfect correspondence between the old, so-called pre-critical gullibility and today's supposedly-critical, but in fact pseudocritical and pseudorthodox, gullibility. The critical program of the nineteenth and twentieth centuries simply has not yet made its way into the study for historical purposes of the literature at hand.

All scholars I survey work on the premise that if the Talmud says someone said something, he really said it, then and there. That premise moreover dictates their scholarly program, for it permits them to describe, analyze and interpret events or ideas held in the time in which that person lived. Some of these would deny the charge, and all of them would surely point, in their writing, to evidence of a critical approach. So I shall show, point by point, that the premise of their articles (these people rarely write books) remains the old gullibility. Specifically, the questions they frame to begin with rest on the assumption that the sources respond. The assumption that, if a story refers to a second century rabbi, then the story tells us about the second century, proves routine. And that complete reliance merely on the allegations of sayings and stories constitutes gullibility: perfect faith in the facticity of fairy-tales. That is gullibility, not a new kind but a very old kind. The only difference? The current generation of scholars claims to know better -- and should know better. The results, furthermore, attract the interest of scholars in adjacent fields, New Testament, early Christianity, ancient history and classics, for instance. But the newest practitioners of gullibility *redivivus* cannot work on the subjects of their choice if they confront the critical program of the day. So they generally pretend to accept that program, while in fact ignoring it. In this respect the old fundamentalists showed greater candor. These judgments cannot make any reader happy; they do not give me joy in writing them. But the scholars' words themselves in every case prove my judgment accurate, indeed moderate. The judgments invariably pertain to what people say, not who or what they are, which is not at issue. *At issue is the work people have published* -- and then in a period of twelve months, mainly in 1984. In citing and criticizing specific statements, to be sure, however, I do not question the learning, credentials, morals, intelligence, professional competence, or integrity of any person. I criticize specific statements, use of evidence, method, premise – those alone.

Writing this book, with its simple indictment, gave me no joy, and reading it will bring to the reader little pleasure. Few felicities of style, profound aperçus, imaginative or illuminating or stimulating observations will serve to relieve the dreary parade of credulous piety and gullible nonsense we are about to witness. This is what people did, not in *yeshivas* in Poland in 1784 or 1885 but in seminaries and universities in New York, Cambridge, Los Angeles, and the State of Israel, in 1984 and 1985. These articles appeared not in distant Jerusalem, with its own politics and its own scholarly canon, but in otherwise reputable scholarly journals.

My interior intent therefore is to restate the question of method in one aspect alone. Let me state it as emphatically as I can:

How do you know exactly what was said and done, that is, the history that you claim to report about what happened long ago? Specifically, how do you know he really said it? And if you do not know that he really said it, how can you ask the question that you ask, which has as its premise the claim that you can say what happened or did not happen?

Jacob Neusner

Program in Judaic Studies
Brown University
Providence, Rhode Island

17 Tishre 5746
October 2, 1985

Acknowledgements

In considerable measure this book goes over old work of mine. That is entirely appropriate, since my point is that nothing but conventional rhetoric has changed in the past quarter-century. Accordingly, I have to prove that the contemporary fundamentalism is no different from the received kind. Hence my surveys of scholarship on the Pharisees and Eliezer ben Hyrcanus demand a rehearing. For people do not realize that what retrograde younger scholars now do is pretty much what true believers did a hundred years ago. The same false (or at least, undemonstrated) epistemological premises endure. Since, furthermore, I wish to place into context the framing and asking of historical questions, I review arguments I worked out a decade ago. What is completely fresh is the operative chapter, on the old fundamentalism *redevivus*. My revisions of the materials published fifteen or more years ago of course are substantial; for one thing I have done a great deal of cutting. But I did want the exact words of the earlier generation to stand alongside those of the current crop of true believers. So I have to include sizable quotations from both generations of believers.

Preface: all new.

Prologue: all new.

Introduction: all new.

Chapter One: substantially revised from "History and the Study of Talmudic Literature" which I presented as the Allan Bronfman Lecture of Shaar Hashomayim Synagogue, Montreal, on November 8, 1978, the Hill Professor's Lecture at the University of Minnesota, Minneapolis/St. Paul, November 15, 1978, and the Tenth Anniversary Plenary Lecture of the Association for Jewish Studies, Boston, Massachusetts, December 17, 1978, and then printed in *Method and Meaning in Ancient Judaism* (Missoula, 1979: Scholars Press for Brown Judaic Studies), pp. 41-58.

Chapter Two: recast and considerably revised from *The Rabbinic Traditions about the Pharisees before 70* (Leiden, 1971): E. J. Brill, III, pp. 321-360.

Chapter Three: revised and abbreviated from *Eliezer ben Hyrcanus: The Tradition and the Man* (Leiden, 1973: E. J. Brill), II, pp. 249-286. I have drastically reduced the discussion to those points urgent for the present book. Readers are invited to refer to the bibliographical essay for a more elaborate account.

Chapter Four: all new (alas!).

Chapter Five: all new.

My thanks go to William Scott Green, with whom I discussed every detail of this book and who gave much valuable advice, and Joshua Bell, *Verbatim,* my word-processor, who has served as my teacher in what I find the second most engaging intellectual adventure of my life, following in line only the Talmuds.

Prologue

Gullibility about Scripture in Current Scholarship

"I want to focus instead on what happened in Egypt."
Michael Walzer

So states the author of *Exodus and Revolution*, an appropriate place to begin our account of reading and believing. For the one thing that the Book of Exodus does not tell us is what happened in Egypt. Walzer confuses the topic of ancient tales with the circumstance to which those tales attest, the simplest error of basic historical research. Exodus tells us what diverse people, long after the events depicted in that mosaic of materials, imagined -- and leads us into that imagination.

Since this book concerns gullibility in the reading of ancient texts, let us begin with Scripture and show the prevailing attitude of mind among believers and scholarly professionals: contemporary scholars who bring to Scripture not their scholarship but their deepest human convictions. In that way the issues of my own field may find a hearing among people more familiar with other fields of religious study than the area of formative Judaism. What we shall see is a prevailing gullibility and how it manifests itself in a certain kind of biblical studies. When we turn to the examination of the corpus of writings of the Judaic sages of late antiquity, readers will have a clear picture of what is at issue. Since Walzer thinks that Exodus tells him what happened in Egypt, he exhibits in his premises precisely that gullibility that, as we shall see in Chapters Two, Three, and Four, characterizes nearly all modern and contemporary scholars of the study of Judaism in its formative centuries. And the consequences, as we shall see here for biblical studies and in Chapter Four for rabbinic studies, prove considerable. For at issue is not whether, but how we shall read the documents at hand for historical purposes: not merely "history," but what kind of history.

To make clear the issues as I see them, I begin with the counterpart program of biblical studies, which is familiar to a broad audience. Then what is under debate in studies of the arcane literature at hand will prove entirely accessible -- and important. I refer to two current works by political scientists. One is Michael Walzer, *Exodus and Revolution* (N.Y., 1985: Basic Books), the other Aaron Wildavsky, *The Nursing Father. Moses as a Political Leader* University,

1984: University of Alabama Press). Wildavsky and Walzer think we can open ancient stories and learn modern lessons. My view is that if we ask narrowly historical questions of documents that do not concern history at all, we violate the lines of order, structure, and meaning that make those documents cogent and important. We ignore all questions of context and circumstance. So the cost of gullibility we pay not only after, but also before the fact. Reading and believing what we read may well mean we cannot even read.

Before we approach Walzer and Wildavsky, let me explain what I mean by the context of a story, and why I think that context makes a difference in our understanding of the content of a story. Using Moses as our example, we turn to stories told about Moses and ask how knowledge of the setting of that story dictates our understanding of the story. In fact, what conclusions should we draw from the knowledge of the world in which a story-teller told a story and in which an audience heard that story? Let me rapidly give three examples of how that fact affects the stories about Moses, one pertaining to Exodus's Moses, the other two to Deuteronomy's Moses. I use as my authority not scholarly literature but a textbook that conveys the firm consensus of biblical learning on the texts at hand.

Moses in the Time of Solomon: In the time of king Solomon, people looked backward to account for the great day at hand. This writer, who flourished around 950 B.C., is known by the name of God that he used in his stories, the Yahwist. He wanted to tell the story of the federation of the federated tribes, now a single kingdom under Solomon, with a focus on Zion and Jerusalem, the metropolis of the federation. What he did, then, was to tell the history (theology) of Israel from its origins, and he made the point that the hand of Yahweh directed events. What he wanted to know out of the past was the present and future of the empire and monarchy at hand.[1] The Yahwist told the story of the creation of the world to the fulfillment of Israel in the conquest of the land. His purpose overall was to affirm that what happened to Israel -- its move from a federation of tribes to an empire under David and Solomon -- was the doing of God, whom he called Yahweh. Lee Humphrey summarizes: "The Israel of the empire was Yahweh's creation for which Yahweh had a mission." The writer lays great emphasis on how God chose a particular person to carry out the mission: Abraham and Sarah, Isaac, Jacob, and onward -- all appeared unworthy and weak, but God chose them. The message, as Lee Humphrey paraphrases it, is this: "The Yahwist focussed attention on just one man, then on twelve sons, then on a band of slaves in Egypt, then on fugitives in Sinai's wastes. Repeatedly endangered, seemingly about to vanish on many occasions, small, weak, and often unworthy, these ancestors of the Israelite empire of David and Solomon were sustained again and again, even in the land of the god-king

---

[1] I follow the excellent and clear account of W. Lee Humphreys, *Crisis and Story: Introduction to the Old Testament* (Palo Alto, 1979: Mayfield Publishing Co.), pp. 65-78.

pharaoh, because they were a chosen people, elected by a god who upheld and preserved them." That is the message.

The Yahwist's picture reduces the covenant at Sinai to modest propositions; the legal stipulations are few (Humphrey, p. 76), focussed in Exodus 34. The patriarchs take priority, the unconditional quality of the promises of God to Abraham -- and later to David -- dominates throughout. At issue then is the promises to the patriarchs and their children, not the contract between God and Israel. Israel is destined by divine grace for its present glory, in Solomon's time. So for the Yahwist, Moses is a minor figure relative to the patriarchs. And what is important about Moses is not the giving of law but the narratives of leadership, Exodus 1-24, 32, 34. And, it follows, *these we read as testimonies to the mentality of the Davidic monarchy.* So, the consensus concurs, when we tell the tale of the Golden Calf, the breaking of the tablets, and the forgiveness of God as an act of grace, we listen to sublime narratives told in the age of Solomon and to the world of Solomon: God's grace favoring Israel in an age cognizant of grace, a powerful message to a self-confident empire

Moses in the Time of Josiah: Does the fact that the Yahwist's Moses speaks to the imperial age of Solomon make a difference? It surely did to the author of Deuteronomy, who gives us a different Moses. If we turn to the book of Deuteronomy, we find a very different picture from the picture we get in Exodus. Now there is a magnificent sermon, preached by Moses before his death, as a narrative of Israel's history. That sermon forms the setting for an enormous law code. At the heart of matters is this claim: here is God's law, which you will keep as your side of the contract that God made with you in bringing you out of Egypt and into the promised land. Moses now serves to validate the laws of the book at hand, that is, of Deuteronomy.

Deuteronomy came to light toward the end of the seventh century, at about 620 B.C., forty years prior to the destruction of the first Temple of Jerusalem. What had happened in the period of the writing of Deuteronomy? Israel had spent a whole generation under Assyrian influence, and only now emerged from that sphere of cultural influence. It sought some other mode of defining itself and its life. It was part of a larger shaking of the foundations, as diverse people, finding in decay the political system that had long stood firm, began to ask about their own distinct and distinctive pasts. Some important segments of the book of Deuteronomy, particularly the legal ones, chapters 12-26, turned up at just this time. These chapters formed roots for the renewed, now independent Israel, of 620. A point of stress in these chapters is that in Jerusalem and only there Yahweh may be worshipped; only the priests of Jerusalem are valid. So the book of Deuteronomy in its earliest layer makes two points: first, one can worship only Yahweh, and, second, one can worship Yahweh only in Jerusalem. Moses then forms the authority for the story -- the authority, but not the leading actor. That is the first part of the story. But Deuteronomy answers a critical question, and, when the document reaches its final stage, forms part of a massive history of Israel, encompassing the books of Deuteronomy, Joshua, Judges, Samuel and Kings. That great work of historical narrative came into being, in its final composition, to answer a question of life and death: why have these things happened to us? The past must live again to explain the present and secure the future. We miss the full meaning of the story if we assume the story-teller addressed the age of "Moses." He spoke of Moses but he meant his own monarch.

Moses and the Destruction of the First Temple: A second phase in the unfolding of the tale of the Deuteronomistic historians took place after the destruction of the Temple in 586. Then Moses would again serve, now to provide the authority for an explanation of the entire history of ancient Israel, culminating, as it had, in the tragedy at hand. Now Moses is law-giver, and the laws form the contract between Israel and God. Israel has violated that covenant or contract, and the result, the destruction, is at hand. Again Humphrey (p. 146): "In Judah and Jerusalem some would turn back to Moses, attempting to redeem the crisis of 587 B.C. [when the Temple was destroyed] by placing it in the theological framework of the old federation story of Israel's origins, for only in this way could Israel's tragic end be understood as the harsh but just action of its god Yahweh. In Moses, who had led Israel from Egyptian slavery, who had mediated the covenant on Mount Sinai, and whose death before the promise of land had been fulfilled had given an effective symbol to Israel's tragically unfulfilled promise, they found a mirror in which to view their own experience. This group found their charter in the book of Deuteronomy, which received its final form at their hands. From this base they reviewed Israel's history from the entrance into Canaan to the exile in Baby after 587...They produced an extended theological survey of Israel's history that now comprises the books of Joshua through 2 Kings. Their book is called the deuteronomistic history because the basis for judgment is found in Deuteronomy." So the Moses of Deuteronomy is a great preacher and gives a sermon on the plains of Moab. The "Moses" at hand projects out of a secure past an account of the later issues and problems and doubts (Humphrey, p. 147). In Deuteronomy Moses says a great deal and does much less, in the Yahwist chapters of Exodus, Moses does much but gives few laws. So the contrast is clear.

What happens when we read the Moses of Deuteronomy in context is that we see each of the details of the picture -- the sermon, the laws -- as a statement to a particular group of people at a particular time. These statements -- admonitions, laws -- take on concreteness. We understand who speaks, we can describe the message, we know the purpose of the whole -- so we understand the matter at its depth. What happens when we ignore context is that we hear only the admonition and the laws and find ourselves able to say little about them in their original setting. The cost is that we do not hear story-tellers telling people of their own age the meaning of what has happened to them -- an enormous message, encompassing the books of Deuteronomy, Joshua, Judges, Samuel, and Kings. Rather, we hear episodic sermons, made up for the occasion, which impose the conditions of a different age and a different world on the magnificent literature at hand.

When we take the Deuteronomistic picture out of its context, of course we join it to the Yahwist's portion of the book of Exodus as well. With what consequence? We join a number of quite diverse stories, each with its own tale to tell, and form them into a conglomerate, the Five Books of Moses as we have them all together, full of points of repetition, contradiction, and incongruity. So we mix pebbles and cookies and ignore the difference -- swallowing the whole thing all at once, choking on nothing. In other words, treating diverse stories as a single story, merely because they refer to a single person, requires us to ignore all manner of detail and contradiction. The Moses who leads the people, so paramount in the Yahwistic picture in Exodus, and the Moses who preaches a majestic sermon and provides a full code of laws, the Moses of Deuteronomy, form one and the same man only in the mind and imagination of people to whom the original stories, their context and meanings, made no difference. And that brings us to the original exercise of harmonization, that is, to the work of the people who sewed the whole into a single cloak, or, to shift the metaphor, who took the pebbles of the Mosaic mosaic and erased the mortar of the margins. But they too had something in mind, and it has no bearing on the discoveries of the political scientists (to whom we shall ultimately return). The framers of the Pentateuch, for their part, had their message to deliver -- also an important one. Then the various Moseses of the antecedent writings formed into a single Moses, as diverse law codes became one, and varied and disharmonious messages from divinities with little in common became the one God who revealed the one unitary Torah to the one man, Moses, at Mount Sinai.

So much for the context of the original stories. What we learn is that Moses served the story-tellers of ancient Israel in whatever way they wanted him to. He was leader, he was law-giver, he stood by himself, he became the figure behind the later history of Israel from the Jordan to Jerusalem and thence Babylon. He was this, he was that, he was the other thing. In context, he emerges as a powerful and important figure, acutely relevant to the context which his diverse creators, the story tellers at hand, defined for him. So much for Moses in context: a set of stories, each formed in judgment of a sequence of circumstances, then all of them joined into a single harmonious message to a critical hour in Israel's history.

From the formation of the Five Books of Moses into a single book the figure of Moses served, as I said at the outset, as a kind of barometer of the cultural climate. From what people said about Moses we learn a great deal about the time and place in which they spoke about Moses. And what we learn about Moses is how his name attracted the fantasies and hopes of the ages. If we wish to understand those fantasies, should we imagine we deal with one man, Moses, and with a single set of events? I think not. In fact we confront a whole set of stories, each with its own context and original point of importance and stress, each represented by its particular Moses. And if we do not ask about context as well as content, we do not grasp content. That is, we do not understand the stress and tension of a story if we totally ignore the setting in which, to the story-teller, those points of stress and tension found resolution and imparted meaning. When we come to the contemporary reading and believing of the Judaic sages writings of late antiquity, we shall look in vain for an interest in the circumstance and context of sayings and stories. What we shall find is speculation on the historical fact within or behind a saying -- a very different thing. That speculation begins in the premise that what matters in a saying or story is its contents -- what it says happened. But in biblical scholarship, we have learned, contents out of context mislead. And, to begin with, the context tells us the fundamental heuristic program at hand: religious or historical, matters of meaning or matters of fact.

If we read Moses in context, we understand the story, its points of stress, its nuances, its generative tensions. Therefore, out of knowledge of context, we know what is at stake in the story, to whom the story matters, what its original meaning conveyed. And why do we want to know the answers to these questions? Because through those answers can identify with the story. By this I mean that we can tell the story in address to an issue, a circumstance, which we, out of our experience, can understand. We can identify with the story not when we turn the story into a tale of ourselves, but when we treat the story as a tale of something beyond ourselves -- but something to which we, too, can relate -- a very different thing. So we locate in our own circumstance those pertinent points of stress and tension that make the story relevant and interesting in its original setting, to its original story teller. So even the aesthetics of the story may speak to us in an authentic way.

If we read Moses out of context, we incur heavy costs. Specifically, we bring to the story of Moses *only* the considerations of our own minds. We impose upon the stories at hand a unity that derives not from their setting -- in the Five Books of Moses, produced in the aftermath of the destruction of the state and of society in 586, -- but from our own. When we bring only ourselves, no information or insight beyond ourselves, we hear in the story only those messages that we did not need the story to convey to us -- that is, only what we knew before. For, without learning, without knowledge of the scholarly tradition on a story, of facts that help us understand the story, the story can only repeat and recapitulate the reality we know, it does not convey the reality to which the authorship addresses itself. Moses out of context tells us only the contents of our own minds, and Moses read in the imaginary and world of our minds -- a single story, not a set of stories, a story that takes place not in real time and among real people and in a real political setting, but only in our imagination -- that Moses teaches us nothing we do not already know. The historical question is not historical at all.

This brings to Walzer and Wildavsky and their gullible reading of Scripture. Walzer in *Exodus and Revolution* treats the stories about Moses as a set of topics, thus "the house of bondage, slaves in Egypt, the murmurings, slaves in the wilderness, the covenant, a free people, the promised land, Exodus politics." His treatment of these topics begins with a biblical tale, and proceeds to broad free-association on the topics at hand. Wildavsky announces his interest very clearly in a chapter, "Why me? why Moses? Why leadership?":

> I am attracted to the study of Moses for many reasons, three of which are related to leadership. The first is that the Mosaic experience is comprehensive, spanning the spectrum of regimes and the types of leadership associated with them. The second is that Moses, far from being beyond us, was full of human faults, from passivity to impatience to idolatry. ...The third is that Moses was a leader who taught his people to do without him by learning how to lead themselves.

Wildavsky further maintains:

> ...understanding of the Mosaic Bible may be enhanced by treating it as a teaching on political leadership; second, that our understanding of leadership may be improved by considering it as an integral part of different political regimes. Moses' experience reveals the dilemmas of leadership under the major types of rule, from slavery in Egypt to anarchy before the golden Calf episode to equity...in the desert, until his final effort to institutionalize hierarchy.

From this program we conclude that the author reads the story as a unitary account of things that really happened. For otherwise he would have to tell us about *how* a given story, told at a given point, addresses problems of leadership *under those circumstances in particular, at that time.* For example, leadership in the time of the Solomonic empire evidently found useful a myth of grace. By contrast, leadership in the time of the breaking up of world empires (for Deuteronomy 12-26), found valuable a myth of totalitarianism: only here, only us. Again, leadership in the time of the destruction of the national polity (for the work of the Deuteronomic historians as a whole) demanded a myth of historical inevitability: the contract, its violation, but also, its potential for renewal. Moses serves all these myths, of course, and Wildavsky can have learned from biblical scholarship interesting lessons for sociology and politics (to name one splendid figure among many, Max Weber has shown how to study these matters for the interests of social science).

But seeing the diverse tales about "Moses" as a single unitary picture, Wildavsky can find in them that "spectrum of regimes and types of leadership" that he does. And why not, when, after all, what he sees as a "spectrum of regimes and types of leadership" is nothing other than a diverse set of stories, written by different people, at different times, for different purposes, and to make different points! All this Wildavsky rips out of context. Any other route would have demanded work -- serious learning -- and not the exercise of powers of free-association and undisciplined imagination.

Does it matter that Wildavsky treats as harmonious and unitary, in a context all its own, a set of tales that, in fact began in bits and pieces? The answer is yes and no. If he performs an act of mere literary criticism, for instance, writing about Don Quixote as an example, in fiction, of such and such an ideal of life, then I think Wildavsky is right. For Moses as a single person, who lived out, in one lifetime, the pastiche of tales about the person named Moses, is a work of fiction. If Wildavsky were to turn, for example, with the same set of questions about the nature of leadership to Shakespeare's *Coriolanus* or *Macbeth*, he would provide an interesting account of Shakespeare's political theory. But he would not tell us much about the nature of leadership in Plutarch's Rome, or in Scotland in earlier times. Then what he would tell us is Shakespeare's theory of politics and leadership in Coriolanus, or even of women in politics (!), in Macbeth. But Wildavsky does not promise a picture of how a writer in the time of Solomon imagined political leadership -- and that we do know. Nor does he tell us how a write in the aftermath of the catastrophe of the destruction of the first Temple reflected on political leadership -- and that we do know. What we know he does not know, and what we do not know he wants to turn into knowledge and insight for political science.

Wildavsky brings to the text only what he finds in the text, reading the whole out of its context in real life, I mean, in diverse ages of material history and concrete society. One could in his defense claim that he proposes to read the stories as structuralists might, but Wildavsky claims no such sophistication. His is not the debate between Marxist reading of literature in the social context and structuralist reading of literature out of all material setting. He comes to the stories with a childlike faith in them. And he reads the stories out of his projection of himself onto them. That is why he treats as facts of real life what is nothing more than the invention of the people who pieced the whole together. To state matters simply: Wildavsky takes a document sewn together in the aftermath of an awful crisis at the end of a nation's life and reads it as the story of the *beginning* of that nation's life! One might as well treat Thomas More's *Utopia* as an account of the politics of a real place and a real time and write a book on political leadership in Utopia.

For his part Walzer announces program far less naive than Wildavsky's. He approaches:

> an idea of great presence and power in Western political thought, the idea of a deliverance from suffering and oppression...I have sought to describe the origins of that idea in the story of Israel's deliverance from Egypt, and then to give a reading of Exodus, Numbers, and Deuteronomy designed to explain their importance for generation after generation of religious and political radicals. The escape from bondage, the wilderness

journey, the Sinai covenant, the promised land: all these loom large in the literature of revolution.

I find this, on the face of it, plausible. For Walzer does not pretend to talk about the stories in their context; he brings his own context for the interpretation of the materials at hand. It is the effect of the stories about Moses among many later generations.

Would that Walzer had remembered, as he wrote the book, his original program. But he moves from tracing the impact of stories on diverse generations backward to the events themselves. For Walzer wishes to do more than study how later generations received Moses. He confesses, "I want to pursue these imaginings, for they illuminate both the ancient books and the characteristically modern forms of political action...So I move back and forth between the biblical narrative...and the tracts and treatises, the slogans and songs, of radical politics..." Walzer says the right thing, but then -- forgetting his fine program -- does the wrong one. On the one hand, Walzer does not pretend to know what actually happened. He distinguishes the story from history: "The story is more important than the events." But the story constitutes an event, with a history of its own. At the same time, we have to ask at what point the story takes on a life of its own. Do we say "Moses did"? Then we use language that suggests we do know what really happened. Do we say, "The story says..."? Then we ask, which component of the story, and, more important, at the hands of which group of story tellers? Walzer in no way grasps that fact. For he defines as his story not this bit and that piece -- nor even the picture of the whole deriving from the aftermath of 586. *He tells the story in the setting of which it speaks, not in the context from which it emerged.* So Walzer takes up the story as a whole, with a beginning, a middle, and an end: problem, struggle, resolution, Egypt, wilderness, promised land (pp. 10-11). But we have a reasonably solid idea of who told that story as a whole, with is beginning, middle, and end, and where and when. Scholarship in general concurs that the story reached its present condition in the aftermath of the destruction of the first Temple. Then we hear a story not about Egypt, wilderness, promised land, from people who are in the wilderness but about those who are returning to the promised land. Walzer has chosen to deal with the story *pretty much as it is told in Scripture* .

When, for example, he says, "A political history with a strong linearity, a strong forward movement, the Exodus gives permanent shape to Jewish conceptions of time," I wonder whatever he can mean, e.g, by "Jewish." Does he mean Jewish conceptions of time in the Judaism that flourished from antiquity to modern times? Then where does he find them? In the definitive Judaic literature of late antiquity, conceptions of time are not at all linear; they keep referring back to ideal time, specifically, in Genesis, at the creation and at the formation of the family of Israel, the Jewish people. In that sense they keep alluding to the cyclicality of time. How so? Israel now, in the fourth century (I refer to the conception of time and of history in Genesis Rabbah) lives out the lives of the patriarchs and matriarchs of Genesis. What happened to them happens now. The deeds of the one form paradigms for the other, not in a moral or ethical sense alone, but in a concrete historical sense. The framers of Genesis Rabbah and Leviticus Rabbah, at the end of the fourth century, interpreted the epochs of world history as recapitulations of the epochs of biblical history in the books of Genesis and Leviticus (but not Exodus, Numbers, and Deuteronomy, a fact that would have impressed Walzer had he done his homework). That theory of recapitulation is not "a linearity of time," and that is not a strong forward movement. It is just the opposite. Walzer knows nothing of this. He has chosen to read the book of Exodus out of its context *and also out of the context of Judaism,*. When Walzer speaks of "Jewish conceptions of time," he is pretending to know things that no one knows, because no one has shown what these are; there is no critical work known to me on the diverse conceptions exhibited by various Judaisms. A page later (pp. 13-14) he appeals to linearity in an appropriate way: "The appeal of Exodus history to generations of radicals lies in its linearity." Now that is a separate thing, I would assume even a valid statement. That statement stands on its own, as a fact, in the way in which the statement on the conception of time in Judaism is no fact at all.

Walzer says, "I want to focus instead on what happened in Egypt." *But the book of Exodus does not tell us what happened in Egypt.* It tells us stories people told about what happened in Egypt. The context of those stories allows us to read them as cultural artifacts (so I argue in Chapter Five for the literature of the Judaic sages of late antiquity). Nothing in those stories suggests we can tell, from them, things that really happened or did not happen. Walzer will look in vain for a scholar of Exodus who thinks that the face of it, the details of the story require us to find out what was going that dark night in Egypt. What does the story tell us? It tells us what the Yahwist thought happened, and the Yahwist made up the stories in the time of Solomon. So if Walzer tells us what happened in Egypt on the basis of what he reads in Exodus, then he might as well tell us on the basis of *A Man for All Seasons* what was going on in the state and church of England in the time of Henry. Or he might as well insist that we cannot read *A Man for All Seasons* unless we know what was going on in twelfth century England -- or unless we ask Richard Burton what he was thinking in those days (to close the matter at its absurd end). The cost proves considerable. We do not hear what the story *does* tell us, which is how people used their minds and imaginations to create a past commensurate with the present they perceived. But we do hear what the story does *not* tell us, which is what happened in Egypt. We will not take seriously the great work of imagination represented by Deuteronomy's centerpiece, the chapters that respond to the breaking up of the old empires. We will not bring sympathy and understanding to the enormous exercise of the Deuteronomic historians in bringing comfort to their people in the aftermath of catastrophe. None of this do we wish to hear. But it is what the Scriptures tell us.

Moses serves not as a fiction of the imagination of political scientists looking for proof-texts or for their own roots, though I hope they find them. "Moses" stands for the work of the creative minds of real people, facing real problems and showing us how they used their powers of imagination to solve those problems. That is why I argue in favor of reading Moses in his context, whether in Solomon's time, or in the age of the destruction of the first Temple in 586. That is when Moses really lived and led his people. That is when he counts. That is why he counts. That is not the only age in which he lived and the only reason that he mattered. But that is the point of entry into the stories. For where and when they were told, the context in which they were important -- these define, to begin with, the traits of the story that would exercise power afterward. It is a fact that someone made up this story, and here is how that person imagined things to be. It is a fact that, through the ages, masses of men and women have responded to these stories. That is a fact worth studying, would that Walzer had remained true to his professed intent of studying it and telling us about it. But he studies Moses and Egypt and purports to know about Judaism and "the Jewish idea of time." The story from Deuteronomy through Kings tells us how diverse thinkers looked back on a history now over but also looked forward to they knew not what. Moses served as the beginning, explaining what would happen in the end. He therefore delivered a message critical to a generation that lived through the end and faced the task of explaining it and thereby surviving. I see this reading of "Moses" as a human achievement of extraordinary power. Moses brought salvation -- if not in Egypt, then, at least, in Babylonia. So much for reading the Bible and believing everything pretty much as it is laid out. Onward, now, to late antiquity and the more subtle modes of gullibility its specialists exhibit.

Introduction

The humanities are fields that do have internal standards...the humanities are a body of ideas, texts, and knowledge of lasting significance, as well as a set of analytical skills that transcend the fields in which they are initially learned.

Richard Ekman
"The Feasibility of Higher Education Reform in the Humanities," *Liberal Education* 71, 1985, p. 274

If the humanities work out propositions in line with shared standards, producing ideas that people can test through rigorous analysis and argument, and generating discourse resting on principles that are learned and therefore shared, the study of the history of the Jews and Judaism in antiquity does not prove it. Why not? This book demonstrates that vulgar gullibility thrives in the study of ancient Judaism. By vulgar gullibility in the instance of specific statements cited here, I mean the conviction that without sustained analysis we can believe pretty much everything the sources record. It precludes civil discourse at all, credulity beyond all argument. Scholarship that paraphrases the sources, learning that records only scholars' beliefs, not their reasons susceptible to proof or disproof through reasoned argument -- that is what today characterizes the generality of learning in ancient Judaism in its formative age, the first through the seventh centuries A.D. I shall prove it by citing exemplary and acutely contemporary statements, published in reputable journals or in books issued by distinguished academic presses.

The generality of these scholarly writings rests on false premises as to the character of the evidence and therefore asks the wrong questions and produces worthless answers. The burden of my indictment is that total gullibility about what ancient sources tell us, incapacity critically to analyze those sources, presently characterize the use, for historical purposes, of the documents of Judaism in late antiquity. Believing Jews of Orthodox or Conservative or Reform, or secular origin, whether young or old, use these sources in ways in which no reputable scholar of the Old or New Testaments would condone in the scholarly reading the biblical writings. Eminent scholars take for granted that we may ignore the entire critical program of biblical learning. So the study of ancient Judaism in its formative centuries produces results in no way based on the principles of scholarship universally honored.

Can we draw an analogy to how things would be done in biblical studies if the same epistemological premise governed? Indeed we can. Working along the same lines, in like manner Old Testament scholars would analyze tales of conversations between Moses and Aaron or Pharaoh as if they really took place, and not as the imaginary compositions of great writers of religious fiction. The scholars, young and old, from whom we shall hear at some length, invoke arguments from the *plausibility* of the contents of a statement for the veracity of that statement. New Testament scholars following that program would tell us that Jesus really made such-and-such a statement, because it sounds like something he would say. So the *"if-I-were-a-horse,-I'd-like-to-eat-oats-too"* school of anthropology finds company in the great stables of Jewish scholarship. The scholars under discussion furthermore invoke the claim that they can identify the point of origin of a statement, without also telling us how we would know if we were wrong. The works of scholarship under discussion recapitulate the mode of historical thought of the Talmud -- "since this statement uses this language, it must have been said before such and such a point, after which such language cannot have been used." So they blunder into minefields of pure guesswork. An analogy in biblical studies? In like manner, biblical scholars would tell us that such and such a proposition has the ring of truth; or "if such and such a proposition is true, then we can solve a further problem," or, "since text X knows nothing of the rule in text Y, therefore text X must come before text Y." That may be so -- but not on the basis of argument alone. At some point, evidence must make its contribution, not to mention tests of falsification and verification. Otherwise we shall never know whether we are right. Deductive logic untested by evidence and unchallenged by skeptical analysis rules supreme.

To state matters simply: if biblical history were written the way the history of the Jews and Judaism in late antiquity (which used to be called "Talmudic history") is written today, the histories of ancient Israel would begin with the creation of the world -- in six days, of course. If complete indifference to the history of the writings in hand were to characterize New Testament scholarship, as that indifference governs Talmudic-historical scholarship, we should be reading more and more harmonies of the Gospels. For the recognition that the four Evangelists preserve viewpoints distinctive to themselves should never have shaped the interpretation of the Gospels, and we should be left with ever more complicated restatements of the Diatesseron.. New Testament scholars know full well that when they come to the rabbinic sources, they tend to use it in ways in which they do not utilize the New Testament. But, as I shall now show, they may take comfort in the simple fact that since the specialists in the Talmudic writings read the documents in a fundamentalist way, the New Testament scholars do no worse. Nonetheless, both Old and New Testament scholarship, with its keen interest in questions of formulation and transmission of sayings, composition of sayings into documents, preservation of mind to which I shall now point. *In contemporary Judaic studies, we routinely deal with premises last found plausible in biblical studies more than one hundred and fifty years ago.*

Where do we start? It is not with the present but the past. In Chapter One, I explain why Judaic scholars of the history of the Jews and Judaism thought that Talmudic literature, that is, the canon of Judaism in late antiquity should serve as a source for historical study. Then, in Chapters Two and Three, I turn to the way things were done before Judaic studies moved into universities, on the one side, and into the critical arena of learning, on the other. In that way I first display the traits of the received gullibility, that is to say, its manifest gullibility, its credulous acceptance of whatever the texts say as so. For that purpose we review what the older generation of scholars, for a long, dreary century, between ca. 1850 and 1970, had to say about two important matters, first, description of a sect, namely, the Pharisees, second, composition of a biography, specifically, Eliezer ben Hyrcanus's. The methods commonly used today in these two enterprises of description will prove entirely familiar to working scholars. So the contrast between what people did and what we now do will be clear.

In Chapter Two I choose the description of a sect because that topic of study runs parallel to writings on the early church. So New Testament scholars can draw their own inferences from observing the use of the sources at hand: is this how *they* utilize statements in the Gospels when they propose to write about the Christian Church of the first and second centuries? If not, why not? So the Pharisees come under description as a parallel to one important topic of learned study among scholars of the same time and region.

In Chapter Three I choose biography because, of course, scholars from the beginning of modern biblical studies have attempted to write biographies, specifically, if not lives of Moses, then at least lives of Jesus. Lives of Jesus produced by academic scholars rarely assign to Jesus everything all the canonical (and non-canonical!) Gospels attribute to him, nor do the authors paraphrase miracle-stories and present them, shorn of the supernatural, as history. Nor do the scholars paraphrase pretty much everything at hand, combine it all into a picture of their own liking, and call it a life of a real person, who really said and did the things attributed to him. But as we shall see, even contemporary scholarship does exactly that.

Chapter Four is the heart of this book. What do I wish to prove? It is a simple proposition:

The single premise characteristic of every scholarly work I shall cite is that if a source says Rabbi X said something, he really said it.

Without that premise, not a single paragraph I shall present can have been conceived and written. If we did not know in advance that whatever is assigned to an authority represents a view held by that person in the time in which, in general, we assume that person lived, none of the scholars at hand can have formulated and asked the questions that they ask and provided the answers they give. Since that premise is manifestly unacceptable as the starting point of historical scholarship, which always starts by asking *how* ancient writers know what they tell us and analyzes sources and their usefulness prior to framing questions, for instance, reporting what really happened, it must follow that all of the work I shall survey is, from a critical-historical viewpoint, a mere curiosity.

Part One

HISTORICAL STUDY OF THE SOURCES OF ANCIENT JUDAISM

Chapter One

The Canon of Judaism as a Historical Source

i

The Study of Talmudic Literature
For Historical Purposes

The study of the Talmud (and the larger canon of writings for which the Talmud stands) for historical purposes has been in three parts: first, use of the Talmudic evidence for the study of the general history of the Near and Middle East of its own times;[1] second, use of historical methods for the study of what was happening among the Jews and especially the people who created the Talmud itself;[2] third, use of historical perspectives in the analysis and elucidation of the Talmud's own materials.[3] None of these three methods has attracted a great number of practitioners. In the concluding section I shall explain why use of historical methods for the study of the world of the Talmud has, on the whole,

---

[1]Historians of the Near and Middle East who have turned to Talmudic materials as a routine part of their examination of the sources are not numerous. In general, well-trained Semitists will be apt to turn to the Talmudic corpus more readily than Classicists and Byzantinists, for obvious reasons. Still, I cannot point to a single major work on the history of the region from Alexander to Muhammed which intelligently and sustainedly draws upon Talmudic evidence. As a general overview, though, I recommend F. E. Peters, *The Harvest of Hellenism. A History of the Near East from Alexander the Great to the Triumph of Christianity* , (New York: Simon and Schuster, 1970).

[2]All the historians of the Jews of this period, by contrast, draw extensively upon the Talmud's evidence. But most of them draw solely upon that evidence. The best examples of well-crafted historical accounts for the period making ample and, for their day (which has passed), reasonably critical use of the Talmudic evidence are: Salo W. Baron, *A Social and Religious History of the Jews,* Vol II, (New York: Columbia University Press, 1952); Michael Avi-Yonah, *The Jews of Palestine. A Political History from the Bar Kochba War to the Arab Conquest,* (Oxford: Basil Blackwell, 1976); and Mary Smallwood, *The Jews under Roman Rule,* (Leiden: E. J. Brill, 1976). Each volume in my *History of the Jews in Babylonia* (5 vols., Leiden: E. J. Brill, 1965-70) opens with a chapter on the political history of the Jews at a given period in the history of the Parthian and Sasanian dynasties; in these chapters the evidences of the Talmudic stories are brought together with those deriving from other sources entirely: Christian, Iranian, Greco-Roman, and the like. The second chapter of each of those books then deals with the inner political history of the Jewish community, and for this purpose Iranian and Talmudic evidences are utilized as well.

[3]I am inclined to think that historical perspectives have clouded the vision of those who attempt them for exegesis of Talmudic literature. The most ambitious and, consequently, the most unsuccessful such effort at a kind of historical exegesis of the Talmud and its law is in Louis Finkelstein's book on Aqiba. But in this regard he merely carried forward the perfectly dreadful approach of Louis Ginzberg. My reasons for regarding this approach to the exegesis of the law of the Talmud as untenable and the results as capricious and unsystematic are amply spelled out in my Chapter Two. I am able to point to the underlying and generative errors in their approach to the interpretation of the legal materials for historical purposes and in their claim to interpret the legal materials from a historical perspective as well (a totally confused work).

produced results of modest interest for people whose principal question has to do with the discovery of what the Talmud is and means. At this point it suffices to say that the assimilatory process has worked well. The Talmud is nt stranger to historical discourse, just as it is a familiar and routine source for the pertinent philological studies.

A history of the study of the Talmud, from the Talmud's formative period in the first through sixth centuries of the common era down to the present day would provide insight into the intellectual history of Judaism, of which the Talmud is the principal component. It also would give us important facts about the sociology of the Jewish people, the intellectual character of its religious life in diverse dimensions, the nature of the educational and cultural institutions which express and shape that life. The reason is that the conditions of society define the things society wants to know. The shape of the program of study of the inherited monuments of culture is governed by the people who propose to carry out that program and the interests of the people who are supposed to contemplate the results of the work.

If, therefore, we ask how the Talmudic canon was studied, we transform a question of intellectual method, superficially a formal question about traits of logic and inquiry. We find ourselves asking about the world in which Jews lived, the values they brought to the Talmud, and the reasons that moved them to open its pages to begin with. So, as I said, when we contemplate the study of the Talmud, we find ourselves examining the history of the inner life of the Jewish people and, self-evidently, the intellectual history of Judaism. The same is so when we want to know why people turned to the canon of Talmudic writings for historical study. This they did not do before the nineteenth century, but they have addressed historical questions to those writings from the mid-nineteenth century to the present. What do we learn about the historical study of the Talmud and related writings from the fact that that study began in the nineteenth century and not in the tenth or fifteenth or twentieth? The questions with which an account of gullibility in the historical study of the Talmudic canon are these:

First, why to begin with was the Talmudic canon studied as a historical document?

Second, what was the intellectual program of the people who originally decided that the Talmud should be studied as a historical document?

Persuasive answers to these four questions will give us a clearer notion of the context and received tradition of contemporary gullibility in the historical study of the canon of Judaism.

ii

The Beginning of "Talmudic History"

The beginning of the study of the Talmud as history, like the beginnings of nearly all of the methods and ideas of the "Jewish humanities," lies in nineteenth-century Germany. Ismar Schorsch[4] points out that the definition of the modern debate about the Talmud, in mostly historical terms, was supplied in a single decade, the 1850s. Four books were published in less than ten years, which defined the way the work would be done for the next one hundred years. These are Leopold Zunz's publication of Nahman Krochmal's *Moreh nebukhe hazeman* ("guide to the perplexed of our times"), 1851; Heinrich Graetz's fourth volume of his *History of the Jews from the Earliest Times to the Present*, which is devoted to the Talmudic period, 1853; Geiger's *Urschrift und Uebersetzungen der Bibel*, 1857; and Zechariah Frankel's *Darkhe hammishnah* ("ways of the Mishnah"), 1859.[5] These four volumes place the Talmud into the very center of the debates on the reform of Judaism and address the critical issues of the debate: the divine mandate of Rabbinic Judaism.[6]

The Talmudic period defines the arena of the struggle over reform because the Reform theologians made it so. They earlier had proposed that by exposing the historical origins of the Talmud and of the Rabbinic form of Judaism, they might "undermine the divine mandate of rabbinic Judaism."[7] As Schorsch points out, Geiger's work indicates the high water mark of the attach on Rabbinic Judaism through historical study. Krochmal, Graetz, and Frankel present a sympathetic and favorable assessment. In so doing, however, they adopt the fundamental supposition of the Reformers: the Talmud can and should be studied historically. They conclude that there is a history to the period in which the Talmud comes forth. The Talmud itself is a work of men in history. The method of Graetz and of Frankel, therefore, is essentially biographical. One third of Frankel's book is devoted to biographies of personalities mentioned in the Talmud. What he does is collect the laws given in the name of a particular man and states that he appears in such and such tractates, and the like. His card file is

---

[4]Ismar Schorsch, *Heinrich Graetz. The Structure of Jewish History and Other Essays,* (New York: Jewish Theological Seminary of America, 1975), p. 48.

[5]I pay little attention to Geiger in what follows because his work had little influence on the course of Talmudic historiography. The main lines of research followed from Frankel, for biography, and Graetz, for narrative history. Geiger certainly proved not only imaginative but rigorous and critical, in the sources under study here nearly alone in his day.

[6]Ismar Schorsch, *Heinrich Graetz,* p. 48. Historical study also served as an instrument in the attack on Talmudic tradition and defense of Reform Judaism in Poland in the same period.

[7]Ismar Schorsch, p. 48.

neatly divided but yields no more than what is filed in it.[8] What is important is not what he proves but, as I said, what he implicitly concedes which is that the Mishnah and the rest of the rabbinic literature are the work of men. Graetz likewise stresses the matter of great men. Schorsch characterizes his work:

> Graetz tried valiantly to portray the disembodied rabbis of the Mishnah and Talmud as vibrant men, each with his own style and philosophy and personal frailties, who collectively resisted the disintegrating forces of their age....In the wake of national disaster, creative leadership forged new religious institutions to preserve and invigorate the bonds of unity...He defended talmudic literature as a great national achievement of untold importance to the subsequent survival of the Jews.[9]

Now why, in the doing of history, the biographies of great men should be deemed the principal work is clear: the historians of the day in general wrote biographies. History was collective biography. Their conception of what made things happen is tied to the theory of the great man in history, the great man as the maker of history. The associated theory was of history as the story of politics, thus of what great men did. Whether or not the Jewish historians of the "Talmudic period" do well, moderately well, or poorly, the sort of history people did in general I cannot say. The important point is that the beginnings of the approach to the Talmud as history meant biography.

What was unimportant to Graetz, Frankel, and Krochmal, was a range of questions of historical method already thoroughly defined and worked out elsewhere. So the work of Talmudic history was methodologically obsolete by the standards of its own age. These questions had to do with the reliability of sources. Specifically, in both classical and biblical studies, long before the mid-nineteenth century a thorough-going skepticism had replaced the gullibility of earlier centuries. Alongside the historicistic frame of mind shaped in the aftermath of the Romantic movement, there was an enduring critical spirit, formed in the Enlightenment and not to be eradicated later on. This critical spirit approached the historical allegations of ancient texts with a measure of

---

[8]Joel Gereboff, "The Pioneer: Zecharias Frankel" in *The Modern Study of The Mishnah* (J. Neusner, ed.), (Leiden: E.J. Brill, 1973), pp. 59-75. Gereboff concludes as follows:

> For Frankel Rabbi was the organizer and the law-giver. He compiled the Mishnah in its final form, employing a systematic approach. The Mishnah was a work of art; everything was "necessary" and in its place. All these claims are merely asserted. Frankel gives citations from Mishnaic and Amoraic sources, never demonstrating how the citations prove his contentions. Frankel applied his theory of positive-historical Judaism, which depicted Jewish Life as a process combining the lasting values from the past with human intelligence in order to face the present and the future, to the formation of the Mishnah. The Mishnah was the product of human intelligence and divine inspiration. Using their intelligence, later generations took what they had received from the past and added to it. Nothing was ever removed. Frankel's work has little lasting value. He was, however, the first to analyze the Mishnah critically and historically; and this was his importance.

[9] Schorsch, p. 48.

skepticism. So for biblical studies, in particular, the history of ancient Israel no longer followed the paths of the biblical narrative, from Abraham onward. In the work of writing lives of Jesus, the contradictions among the several gospels, the duplications of materials, the changes from one gospel to the next between one saying and story and another version of the same saying and story, the difficulty in establishing a biographical framework for the life of Jesus -- all of these and similar, devastating problems had attracted attention. The result was a close analysis of the character of the sources as literature, for example, the recognition -- before the nineteenth century -- that the Pentateuch consists of at least three main strands: JE, D, and P. It was well known that behind the synoptic Gospels is a source (called Q, for Quelle) containing materials assigned to Jesus, upon which the three evangelists drew but reshaped for their respective purposes.

The conception that merely because an ancient story-teller says someone said or did something does not mean he really said or did it goes back before the Enlightenment. After all, the beginnings of modern biblical studies surely reach into the mind of Spinoza. He was not the only truly critical intellect in the field before Voltaire. But as a powerful, socially rooted frame of mind, historical-critical and literary-critical work on the ancient Scriptures is the attainment of the late eighteenth and nineteenth centuries. And for the founders of Talmudic history, Graetz, Frankel, and Krochmal, what had happened in biblical and other ancient historical studies was either not known or not found to be useful. And it was not used.

No German biographer of Jesus by the 1850s could have represented his life and thought by a mere paraphrase and harmony of the Gospels, in the way in which Graetz and Frankel and their successors down to the mid-twentieth century would paraphrase and string together Talmudic tales about rabbis, and call the result "history" and biography. Nor was it commonplace, by the end of the nineteenth century, completely to ignore the redactional and literary traits of documents entirely, let alone their historical and social provenance. Whatever was given to a rabbi, in any document, of any place or time, was forthwith believed to provide evidence of what that rabbi really said and did in the time in which he lived.

iii

The Theological Motive in "Talmudic History"

By now it is clear that the "Talmudic-historians" did not want to know what the Talmudic canon had to tell them, but did take an interest in matters about which, in fact, the Talmudic writings cannot[10] report: things that really happened, statements really made by the people to whom they are attributed.

---

[10]Perhaps rather: *have not yet been demonstrated to* report. But I do not know how we should demonstrate that we have ipsissima verba, and I spent several major projects trying to find a way. The other side does not face the same problem: they just believe.

Now why these people did what they chose to do is no more important than why they refrained from doing what they chose not to do. Just as they chose to face the traditionalists with the claim that the Talmud was historical, so they chose to turn their backs on the critical scholarship of their own day with the very same claim that the Talmud was historical. I think the apologetic reason is self-evident and requires no amplification. We may now answer our first two questions. The Talmud was first studied as a historical document because, in the war for the reform of Judaism, history was the preferred weapon. The Talmud was the target of opportunity. The traditionalists trivialized the weapon, maintaining that history was essentially beside the point of the Talmud: "The historians can tell us what clothes Rab wore, and what he ate for breakfast. The Talmudists can report what he said." But, it goes without saying, polemical arguments such as these, no less than the ones of the Reformers, were important only to the people who made them up.

The weapon of history in the nineteenth century was ultimate in the struggle for the intellect of Jewry. And the intellectuals, trained as they were in the philosophical works of the day, deeply learned in Kant and Hegel, made abundant use of the ultimate weapon. The Reformers similarly chose the field of battle, declaring the Hebrew Scriptures to be sacred and outside the war. They insisted that what was to be reformed was the shape of Judaism imparted by the Talmud, specifically, and preserved in their own day by the rabbis whose qualification consisted in learning in the Talmud and approval by those knowledgeable therein. But the shape of the subject and its results, paradoxically, also reveal the mind of the traditionalist Reformers, Graetz and Frankel. Their intellectual program consisted of turning the Talmud, studied historically, into a weapon against the specific proposals and conceptions of the Reformers. And for the next hundred years, with only one important additional area of study, the history of the "Talmudic period" would be the story of rabbis, paraphrases of Talmudic and midrashic units strung together with strings of homilies -- where they were strung together at all.

This additional area of study need not detain us for long, for what is done in it is essentially what is done in biography. I refer to the study of what was called "Talmudic theology" or Talmudic thought" or "Rabbinic theology." In English the pioneering work is Solomon Schechter's *Studies in Judaism,* three volumes beginning in essays in the *Jewish Quarterly Review,* 1894 through 1896. The next important work in English is George F. Moore's classic, *Judaism,* published in 1927, then C.G. Montefiore's and H. Loewe's tasteful *Rabbinic Anthology,* 1938, and Ephraim Urbach's, *The Sages. Their Concepts and Beliefs,* in Hebrew in 1969 and English in 1975. (There were parallel works in German as well, none important.) In all of these works the operative method is the same as in biography, but the definitive category shifts to theology. Each work takes up a given theological category and gathers sayings relevant to it.

The paraphrase of the sayings constitutes the scholarly statement. Urbach correctly defines the work which was not done:

> *the history of the beliefs and concepts of the Sages against the background of the reality of their times and environment* (italics his).[11]

The use of evidence for the theological character of Talmudic Judaism is just as gullible and credulous as it is for biographies of Talmudic rabbis. What is attributed to a given rabbi really was said by him. What he is said to have done he really did. No critical perspective is brought to the facts of the Talmud. And the Talmud always supplies the facts, all the facts, and nothing but the facts

We need not dwell on the historical study of the Talmud for theological purposes, therefore, because the methods were not different from those taken to be essentially sound for the study of the Talmud for biographical purposes. And these two purposes -- biography and theology -- define the character of nearly all of the historical work done in Talmudic literature for the century from the decade of foundation onward. Graetz set the style for such history as was attempted; Frankel for biography. The greatest achievements of the next hundred years -- I think of the names of Buechler and Alon, for example[12] -- in no way revised the methods and procedures or criticized the fundamental suppositions laid forth in Graetz and Frankel. When we realize the conceptual and methodological history of biblical studies in that same century, when we gaze upon the stars which rose and the stars which fell, when we remember the fads and admire the lasting progress, we realize that the Talmud as history is a world in which the clock started in 1850 and stopped in 1860. That of course is an exaggeration. Even those who could find no better methods and suppositions than those used for a hundred years could at least propose better questions. A clearly historical, developmental purpose is announced, though not realized, for example, by Urbach, when he says:

> The work of the sages is to be viewed as a protracted process aimed at the realization of the Torah and the ideals of the prophets in the reality and framework of their time....[13]

Now while this is a clearly apologetic and theological proposal, it does make a place for the notion of change and development, that is, a genuinely -- not merely a superficially -- historical proposal. At the end let me quote Schorsch's

---

[11]Ephraim Urbach, *The Sages. Their Concepts and Beliefs* , 2 Vols. (Jerusalem: Magnes Press, 1975), p. 5.

[12]G. Alon, *Toledot hayyehudim be'eres yisra'el betequfat hammishnah vehattalmud* (1954-55). These are uneven, and most of the work on ancient history is seriously out of date.

[13]Ephraim Urbach, *The Sages. Their Concepts and Beliefs* , 2 Vols. (Jerusalem: Magnes Press, 1975), p. 17.

judgment of Graetz, which forms a devastating epitaph to the whole enterprise of Talmudic history from the 1850s to the 1960s:

> Above all, Graetz remained committed to the rejuvenation of his people. His faith in God's guiding presence throughout Jewish history, as witnessed by two earlier instances of national recovery, assured him is the future. His own work, he hoped, would contribute to the revival of Jewish consciousness. He succeeded beyond measure. As a young man, Graetz had once failed to acquire a rabbinic pulpit because he was unable to complete the delivery of his sermon. There is more than a touch of irony in the remarkable fact that the reception accorded to Graetz's history by Jews around the world made him the greatest Jewish preacher of the nineteenth century.[14]

iv
What Has Changed in the Past Quarter-Century

Let me now briefly specify the answers to my third and fourth questions, raised earlier: What is the intellectual program of the people who today do the work? Why is the Talmud studied today as a historical document? Answering these questions requires attention to the setting of the people who do the work. These are all university people. Talmudic history may be taught in some Jewish theological institutions -- not in Yeshivas at all -- but no books or articles in Talmudic history emerge from these schools. The books and articles in this field over the past twenty years have been written by university professors in America and Canada (and even in the State of Israel). The reason this particular aspect of Talmudic studies is important to professors in diaspora-universities should be made clear.

Among those engaged in the teaching of the "Jewish humanities," the Talmud is a particularly important document. It is distinctively Jewish. The Hebrew Scriptures are not; they are a splendid literature and a self-evidently important one. Much of the medieval philosophical and mystical literature is of very special interest. The Talmud, by contrast, speaks of the formative years of Judaism as we know it; and it addresses itself, also, to the centuries in which the two other religions of the West (Christianity, for the earlier phases of the Talmud, and Islam, for the very last phases) were taking shape. Consequently, there is a genuine interest in Talmudic learning among a wide audience of scholars and students. It is natural, therefore, for people in the setting of secular universities to turn to Talmudic studies as a distinctively Jewish, important, and welcomed topic.

But what people in universities want to know has little to do with the ritualistic repetition of hagiography. They are not apt to sit still very long for edifying tales of ancient rabbis (or other sorts of holy men either). There is a contemporary program of research, a set of questions which just now appear

---

[14]Schorsch, pp. 61-62.

urgent and pressing, as much as the issues of the reform of Judaism through historicism appeared urgent and pressing a century ago. Of still greater importance for the present part of the argument, there is a considerable and shared program of criticism, historical, literary, anthropological and philosophical, as well as religionsgeschichtlich. This program is naturally attractive. One question which to New Testament scholars is deemed unavoidable is how to tell what, if anything, Jesus really said among the sayings attributed to him, and what Jesus really did among the deeds assigned to him. There is no way that what is perceived as "gullibility" will find a serious hearing in the study of Judaism when that same attitude of mind is found barbaric and irrelevant in the study of Christianity of the same place and early the same time. It follows, as I indicated at the outset, that the pressing problems of this second century of Talmudic studies for historical purposes are not, Did Rabbi X really say what is attributed to him? but, What do we know if we do not know that Rabbi X really said what is attributed to him? What sort of historical work can we do if we cannot do what Frankel, Graetz, and Krochmal thought we could do?

The effort to recover the biographies of individual rabbis of the late first and early second centuries is not feasible and not interesting. It seems to me that the same conclusion holds for the rabbis who lived in the later second century, since the literary facts pertinent to Aqiba apply without much variation to Judah, Simeon, Meir, or Yose. The state of the question for the rabbis of the third and fourth century is apt to be shaped by the nature of the quite different processes of literary formulation and transmission which produced the Talmuds in which their materials in the main are preserved, on the one side, and those same processes which yield the Midrashic compilations, on the other. These have not been critically assessed in detail, so we cannot yet come to conclusions on the promise of rabbinic biography for the "Amoraic" period. Let me now spell out my claim that Talmudic biography yields no interesting results. We consider the thumbnail biography of Hillel produced by a Jewish New Testament scholar.

v

What Is Wrong with the Historical Reading
of the Talmudic Canon
The Case of Samuel Sandmel

Two kinds of problems in my view call into question the fruitfulness of historical study of the Talmud. It is because of these two problems that I turn to a field other than history to find some useful questions for those many answers which we have at hand. The first problem is obvious. The Talmud simply is not a history book. To treat it as if it were is to miss its point. The second is that when we ask the wrong questions, we miss the answers the Talmud gives us to many right questions. These are two sides to the same coin.

The Talmud and related literature were not created to record things that happened. They are legal texts, saying how people should do things (and, sometimes, do do things); or they are exegetical texts, explaining the true meaning of the revelation at Sinai, in Torah; or, occasionally, they are biographical texts, telling stories about how holy men did things. They are put together with an amazing sense of form and logic, so that bits and pieces of information are brought into relationship with one another, formed into a remarkably cogent statement, and made to add up to more than the sum of the parts. Talmudic essays in applied logic rarely are intended to tell us things which happened at some one point. They still more rarely claim to inform us about things that really happened For, in the end, the purpose of the Talmudic literature, as Talmudists have always known, is to lay out paradigms of holiness. The purpose is to explore the meaning of being human in the image of God and of building a kingdom of priests and a holy people. For that purpose, the critical questions concern order and meaning. The central tension in the inner argument lies in the uncovering of sacred disciplines. The Talmud describes that order, that meaning, which, in society and in the conduct of everyday life, as well as in reflection and the understanding of the meaning of Israel and the world, add up to what God wants. The Talmud is about what is holy. That message does not attract a hearing, but the nonsense about Hillel as gentle and Shammai as irascible does. Those with such selective attention to the source at hand clearly do not respect the source or its authorship. For when they ask historical questions, they simply refuse to listen to the Talmud's message about its world.

Why so? Because in the quest for the holy order, things of interest to historians, that is, the concrete, one-time, discrete and distinctive events of history, present obstacles. For order lies in regularity. But history is the opposite. It is what is interesting, which is what is unusual. That is what is worth reporting and reflection. So it will follow that the last thing of interest to people of the sort of mind who made the Talmud is whether or not things really happened at some point.[15] What they want to know is how things always happen and should happen. If I may project upon the creators of the Talmudic literature what I think their judgment would be, they would regard history as banal. My basis for thinking so is not solely that they wrote so little of it. It is principally that they wrote something else. So history misses the point they wish to make.

---

[15] I stress that this issue is simply beside the point. It is not relevant to Talmudic discourse. Therefore to accuse the rabbis of lying because they tell didactic tales and moral or theological fables, rather than writing history like Tacitus or Josephus, is to miss the point of what the rabbis of the Talmud mean. By their long arguments of analysis and applied and practical reason they propose to bring to the surface underlying unities of being. It is the most naive sort of anachronism to accuse them of being uninterested in truth because they do not record events, or record them in fanciful way, since it denies the logicians their task but expects them to work like historians instead.

Besides the triviality of history and the inappropriate character of its questions, there is yet a further problem, of a quite different order. Readers know this problem well, since it precipitated my writing this book. It concerns how history is done today. For a long time in Western culture we have understood that merely because an ancient source says something happened that does not mean it really happened that way, or even happened at all. An attitude of skepticism toward the claims of ancient documents was reborn in the Renaissance and came to fruition, in the religious sciences, in the eighteenth and nineteenth centuries. From that time onward, it was clearly understood that, in trying to figure out who did what and why, we are going to stand back from our sources and ask a range of questions not contained in them. When we come to the Talmudic sources out of which some sort of history (biography, politics, or a history of ideas) may be constructed, so that we have a sense of what came first and what happened then, we have therefore to reckon with the problem of the accuracy and reliability of our sources. That problem would confront us in the examination of any other source of the period of which the Talmud is a part. It is not an insurmountable problem. But it must be met.

Now when we combine these several problems -- the problem of the intent of our sources and the meaning they wish to convey, the problem of the accuracy of our sources for doing the work which people generally call historical -- we realize that the historical approach to the Talmud requires a considerable measure of thoughtfulness. Studying the Talmud as history demands the exercise of the same restraint, probity, and critical acumen that are routinely required in all fields of ancient studies. Failure to apply them results in a kind of fundamentalist fiction-writing. For example, in his widely-read book, *Judaism and Christian Beginnings*[16] Samuel Sandmel provides an account of what he at the outset admits are "legends" about some of the holy men of the Talmudic literature. But having called the legends legends, he turns them into history. Why do I insist that what Sandmel calls legends in sentence one he treats as historical facts in sentence three? He tells these stories not in a book about the third or fourth or fifth century development of holy men in Christianity and Judaism as mediators of the sacred, but rather, and specifically, in the context of his description of the state of Judaism in the formative century of Christianity. It is self-evident that he would not write about these particular men if he were discussing the Judaism of the third or fourth centuries -- the centuries in which the stories he cites first are attested by the redaction (it is generally assumed) of the documents in which they occur. When, therefore, Sandmel chooses Hillel and Shammai, he clearly wishes the reader to believe that he is telling about people who are contemporaries of Jesus. Sandmel's credulous narrative about Hillel shows that he has treated his "legends" as historical fact:

---

[16]Samuel Sandmel, *Judaism and Christian Beginnings*, (New York: Oxford University Press, 1978), pp. 236-51.

> Hillel loved his fellow man a deeply as he loved the Torah, and he loved all
> literature of wisdom as much as he loved the Torah, neglecting no field of study.
> He used many foreign tongues and all areas of learning in order to magnify the
> Torah and exalt it..., and so inducted his students.[17]

The voice of this paragraph is the historian; nothing is in quotation marks, and footnotes lead the reader to unanalyzed, unquoted source. The language is thus not of analysis but of historical fact.

Now the cited paragraph in fact presents nothing but a paraphrase of materials found in rabbinic sources of a far later age than Hillel's own time. None of the sources emerging from the late second century (a mere two hundred years after Hillel is supposed to have lived) knows about Hillel's vast knowledge. Indeed, in an age in which the sources report conflict on whether or not Jews should study Greek, and in which only a few highly placed individuals are allowed (in the Mishnaic corpus) to do so, no one thought to refer to the "fact" of Hillel's having known many languages. The reason, I think, is that no one knew it, until it was invented for purposes of storytellers in the age in which the story was told, whatever these purposes may have been.[18] If it is the Hillel of legend, then it is a legend which testifies to the state of mind of the storytellers hundreds of years after the time of Hillel (and Jesus).[19] The stories Sandmel tells us on the face of it record absolutely nothing about the age, let alone the person, of Hillel himself.

When Sandmel claims to tell us about the time of Jesus and then arrays before us perfectly routine third-, forth-, or fifth-century rabbinical hagiography, he is engaged in a restatement, as history, of what in fact are statements of the cultural aspirations and values of another age than Hillel's. It was one in which -- in the present instance -- some story-tellers appear to have wanted people to appreciate Torah-learning in a broad and humanizing context (if we may take a guess as to what is at hand in these particular allegations about Hillel). But if, for the turn of the first century, we have evidence that the ideal of Torah-study

---

[17] Samuel Sandmel, p. 237.

[18] I cannot point to a single study of why, in third and fourth century writings but not in earlier ones, the sages of the first and second centuries get biographies that they formerly had lacked. Yet this was the age of biographies in Greco-Roman life in general, and it also was the time that holy men came to prominence as mediators of the sacred. So the age of the documents that present the tales should make a difference -- at least as a matter of hypothesis. But the people will not do the work. It is much easier, after all, to tell fairy stories and impress those Christians, who went to hear them. They are not few.

[19] It is commonplace to allege that there was a continuous process of oral tradition. But no one has proved it in detail, not for all of the documents, not for all of the materials in them. It is a self-serving rationalization for the fundamentalism at hand, not a serious scholarly argument, academically demonstrated through tests of falsification and validation. The argument from oral tradition, asserted but unproved, testifies to self-indulgence among people who in their own area know better. It is one thing to show that a given document indicates that it is formulated to be memorized, as I have proved for the Mishnah. It is another to allege on the basis of stories or sayings that all documents, or all traditions now contained in documents, were memorized. That allegation rests on the generalization of a few stories, treated as absolute fact, about how God taught the Torah to Moses (!), and the like: fundamentalism at a new low.

was not associated with the very movement of which Hillel is supposed to have been part, but of a quite different set of people entirely, then I am inclined to think Sandmel claims the sources present information they do not necessarily contain.

I do not mean to suggest that biography, or the study of lives, promises no interesting results. The sources at hand can tell us provocative things. In the study of the history and character of the traditions in the names of Yavneans, for example, we learn what it was important to say about those authorities in the times in which those responsible for the later compilations did their work. We notice, first of all, that in the third and fourth and later centuries, the telling of stories about earlier rabbis was deemed an important part of the work of traditioning and handing on the Tannaitic corpus. Men who, in their own day and for a century thereafter, are important, e.g., in Mishnah-Tosefta, principally in connection with opinions in their names on mooted topics of Mishnah-Tosefta, now, in the strata of the Talmuds and in the Midrashic compilations require yet another treatment entirely. They must be turned into paragons of virtue and exemplars of the values of the growing rabbinic movement. Long after their legal traditions had come to closure, their "biographies" continue to grow in response to a self-evident need to expand the modes by which Rabbinic tradition would express itself and preserve and impart its teachings. The histories of the traditions of the several authorities of Yavneh prove beyond doubt that it is in the third and fourth centuries that the telling of stories about rabbis of the first and second centuries, the making up of homilies about their deeds, and the provision of a more human visage for the ancient authorities became important to Rabbinic circles of both Palestine and Babylonia.

vi
History in a Different Dimension

If historians do not ask the critical and generative questions, then we have to look for help to those who do. Perhaps the most difficult problem is to overcome our own circumstance, our own intellectual framework. For in thinking the Talmud important, we tend to claim it is important for our reasons. We ask it to address questions interesting to us, without finding out whether these are the right questions for the Talmud too. Let me now spell this problem out.

The distance between this century and the centuries in which the Talmud was brought into being is not simple to measure. It is not merely that the rabbis and most others of their day thought the world was flat, and we know it is not. It is that the way in which they formulated the world, received and organized information about life, profoundly differs from that of our own day. We are not equipped to interpret the Talmud's world-view if we bring to it our own. We drastically misinterpret earlier rabbinic documents when we simply seek places on the established structure of issues and concerns on which to hang whatever seems relevant in the Talmudic literature.

By way of illustration: when the rabbis of the later first and second centuries produced a document to contain the most important things they could specify, they chose as their subjects six matters, of which, I am inclined to think, for the same purpose we should have rejected at least four, and probably all six. That is, the six divisions of the Mishnah are devoted to purity law, tithing, laws for the conduct of sacrifice in the Temple cult, and the way in which the sacrifices are carried on at festivals -- four areas of reality which, I suspect, would not have found a high place on a list of our own most fundamental concerns. The other two divisions, which deal with the transfer of women from one man to another and with matters of civil law -- including the organization of the government, civil claims, torts, and damages, real estate and the like -- complete the list. When we attempt to interpret the sort of world the rabbis of the Mishnah propose to create, therefore, at the very outset we realize that that world in no way conforms, in its most profound and definitive categories of organization, to our own. That is why we need help in interpreting what it is that they propose to do, and why they choose to do it that way and not in some other.

It follows that the critical work of making sense and use of the Talmudic literature is to learn how to hear what the Talmud wishes to say in its own setting and to the people addressed by those who made it up. For that purpose it is altogether too easy to bring our questions and take for granted that, when the rabbis of the Talmud seem to say something relevant to our questions, they therefore propose to speak to us. Anachronism takes many forms. The most dangerous comes when an ancient text seems accessible and clear.[20] For the Talmud is separated from us by the whole of Western history, philosophy, and science. Its wise sayings, its law, and its theology may lie in the background of the law and lore of contemporary Judaism. But they have been mediated to us by many centuries of exegesis, not to mention experience. They come to us now in the form which theologians and scholars have imposed upon them. It follows that the critical problem is to recognize the distance between us and the Talmud.

The second problem, closely related to the first, is the work of allowing strange people to speak in a strange language about things quite alien to us, and yet of learning how to hear what they are saying. (We return to this matter in Chapter Five.) That is, we have to learn how to understand them in their language and in their terms. Once we recognize that they are fundamentally different from us, we have also to lay claim to them, or, rather, acknowledge their claim upon us. The document is there. It is interesting. It is important and fundamental to the definition of Judaism. When we turn to the humanities

---

[20] I think theologians and historians of Talmudic theology most consistently commit the sin of anachronism. In this regard the list of examples covers the bibliography of available monographs and books. I cannot think of a single theologian who begins with consideration of the character of the sources and what he proposes to say about them. Everyone works as if "we all know" what we are doing.

and social sciences of our own day with the question, Who can teach us how to listen to strange people, speaking in a foreign language, about alien things? I am inclined to look for scholars who do just that all the time. I mean those who travel to far-off places and live with alien tribes, who learn the difficult languages of preliterate peoples, and who figure out how to interpret the facts of their everyday life so as to gain a picture of that alien world and a statement of its reality worth bringing back to us. Anthropologists study the character of humanity in all its richness and diversity. What impresses me in their work is their ability to undertake the work of interpretation of what is thrice-alien -- strange people, speaking a strange language, about things we-know-not-what -- and to translate into knowledge accessible to us the character and the conscience of an alien world-view. But this too in the present context defines a labor of historical study. Few historians understand that fact, since to them the study of history simply limits itself to the things historians in particular want to know about the past. That is to say, history is not about everything that is there, but only some of the things that are there.

vii

Conclusion

A sign of a field of study in flux is the incapacity of scholars to find common grounds for disagreement. At the present time the Talmud is read as history in two completely different ways. Those who do it one way cannot communicate with those who do it the other. For example, those who maintain the established theory of the character of the Talmudic sayings and stories as facts of history, pure and simple, will present to those who do not the following arguments: 1) the rabbis were scrupulous about the truth; 2) facts incorrectly reported were challenged; 3) the holy rabbis of the Talmud surely would not lie. To these assertions, a master of the contrary viewpoint -- that Talmudic stories, like biblical ones, have to be read in a critical spirit -- will reply with such words as "sometimes" and "probably." That is, the rabbis *sometimes* were scrupulous about the truth. Facts sometimes were challenged when reported incorrectly. The holy rabbis of the Talmud *probably* would not lie. But, this master will add, "Rabbinic literature is full of obviously contradictory and grossly false statements. Contradictory reports stand unchallenged as often as they are corrected. The rabbinic literature contains innumerable nonsensical and obviously incredible statements." So, this master concludes, "If the rabbis were so scrupulous and painstaking as you pretend, how do you account for the enormous mass of claptrap they handed down?"[21] In fact we hear an argument between two fundamentalists, a pious one and a heretical one. Both believe with all their hearts, one to love, the other to hate. Clearly, an argument phrased in

---

[21]I here paraphrase a correspondence between an American scholar and an Israeli one about the veracity of Talmudic stories about rabbis and attributions of sayings to rabbis. Language in quotation marks is drawn from the actual correspondence.

the language of piety provokes the language of anti-piety, as well it should. But it appears to me that the argument is poorly phrased when the "veracity" of "the rabbis" is made the issue. What really requires attention is the identification of the things we shall concur to regard as facts and the questions to which these facts are claimed to be relevant. An Israeli graduate student (of American origin) who attended a conference at which issues such as those under discussion here were raised made the following comment:

> I am used to historians who argue with one another by showing that the hypothesis suggested by competitors is either contradicted by some know datum or unnecessarily involved or extravagant to explain the known data, as a simpler hypothesis would equally do. That is, everyone assumes that the few known data, which by themselves do not give us an understandable picture, are the surviving fragments of a 'building' which once stood. The historian's job is to suggest what that building looked like.

Now this conception of the writing of history confuses history with mathematics.

But the insight that no longer is there any agreement whatever on what constitutes facts and how facts are discovered and defined is significant. I think it is entirely sound and accurate, not only for the conference on which the student comments, but also for the state of the field of the Talmud as history. That is why the sort of discourse about "the holy rabbis' not telling lies" is possible.[22] For, as I think is clear from the perspective of historical studies, we are not entirely sure what we mean by the truth. That is why we cannot say what is an untruth. We in the humanities do our work in an age of powerful, conflicting currents of thought. There is little agreement on fundamental issues of method and theories of knowledge. It is no wonder that the character of the work done by the end of this first quarter of the second century of the study of the Talmud as history should appear to be diverse and lacking a common core of consensus and concurrence.

---

[22]But this is just an unsophisticated form of the " *they-must-have-had-a-tradition*"- or "...*a reason*" - argument, not to mention the hypothesis of incredibly accurate oral formulation and oral transmission of things that really were said and done. Where is the proof?

Part Two

THE OLD GULLIBILITY

Chapter Two

Describing a Historical Group
The Pharisees

i
Introduction

When in 1971 I wrote my *Rabbinic Traditions about the Pharisees before 70*, I concluded with a survey of as many important (and unimportant) studies on the Pharisees as I could turn up. The result was a forty-page bibliographical appendix, which I have here revised and cut down. The main points of method I give up front, then the survey, drastically abbreviated, follows.

ii
The Syllabus of Errors

The following outline summarizes the chief historical faults found in the materials surveyed above, together with the names of some of the scholars in whose writings those faults are exemplified.

I. **Faulty Scholarship**

    1. Neglect of some of all of the rabbinic traditions about the Pharisees

        a) Houses-materials not used at all

        b) Houses-materials not thoroughly consulted

        c) Rabbinic traditions rejected without close examination

        d) Reliance on secondary accounts of rabbinic traditions

    2. Neglect of non-rabbinic evidences about the Pharisees or materials contained in rabbinic traditions

        a) No reference to archaeological data pertinent to historical interpretation

        b) Failure to follow the development of New Testament scholarship

        c) No consistent reference to Hellenistic literary and cultural parallels

    3. Failure to consult relevant secondary literature

    4. Failure to articulate and examine questionable presuppositions

II. Faulty Use of Evidence

1. Attributions of sayings are always reliable
2. What a story says happened actually did take place (credulousness)
3. Even miracle stories are of historical value in their own terms
4. If the story were not true, why should the tradition have preserved it? Variation: "They must have had a good reason to tell the story"
5. Construction of narrative by paraphrase of rabbinic stories about Pharisees (gullibility, similar to no. 2)
6. Presumption of unitary pericopae
7. Use of emendations of texts to solve historical difficulties
8. Claim of exact chronological or historical accuracy even of fables
9. Invention of historical settings or motives for exegetical materials
10. All versions of a story are correct and must be harmonized and unified (unitary tradition)
11. "No real evidence has been produced against the historicity of the accounts" (similar to no. 4)
12. Evidence contrary to one's theory is ignored
13. All stories deriving from all compilations are equally valid testimonies (parallel to no. 10 -- all pseudocritical scholars

III. Faulty Narrative

1. False, inappropriate, or misleading analogies

Among the historiographical errors of pseudocritical scholars, three are so serious as to render their historical results virtually useless: first, the failure carefully and critically to analyze the literary and historical traits of every pericope adduced as evidence; second, the assumption that things happened exactly as the sources allege; third, the use of anachronistic or inappropriate analogies and the introduction of irrelevant issues. One or more of these three fundamental fallacies may account for every one of the specific faults listed above, as well as for many not specified. The historians might have learned the need for literary- and historical-critical analysis from classical and biblical scholarship of the past century and a half; second, they might have proved less gullible and credulous had they taken seriously the historical and philosophical achievements of the Enlightenment, at least its skepticism; and the study of the history of historical scholarship and of the sociology of knowledge ought to have suggested the dangers of anachronism, moralizing, and didacticism.

iii
Talmudic History and Apologetics:
Talmudism Applied to Historical Studies

The study of Talmudic and related literature for historical purposes stands conceptually and methodologically a century and a half behind biblical studies. While biblical literature has for that long been subjected to the criticism of scholars who did not take for granted the presuppositions and allegations of the text, Talmudic literature was studied chiefly in yeshivot, whose primary interests were not historical to begin with, and whose students credulously took at face value both the historical and the legal sayings and stories of the Talmudic sages. Here the influences of literary and historical criticism emanating from universities were absent. The circle of masters and disciples was unbroken by the presence of non-believers; those who lost the faith left the schools. When Talmudic literature was studied in universities, it was mainly for philological, not historical, purposes. The greatest scholars relied on secondary literature.[1]

Those Talmudists, such as Abraham Geiger and Louis Ginzberg, moreover, who did acquire a university training, including an interest in history, and who also continued to study Talmudic materials, never fully overcame the intellectual habits ingrained from their beginnings in *yeshivot*. Characteristic of Talmudic scholarship is the search, first, for underlying principles to make sense of discrete, apparently unrelated cases, second, for distinctions to overcome contradictions between apparently contradictory texts, and third, for *hiddushim*, or new interpretations of a particular text. That exegetical approach to historical problems which stresses deductive thought, while perhaps appropriate for legal studies, produces egregious results for history, for it too often overlooks the problem of evidence: How do we know what we assert? What are the bases in actual data to justify *hiddushim* in small matters, or, in large ones, the postulation of comprehensive principles (*shitot*) of historical importance? Ginzberg's famous theory that the disputes of the Houses of Shammai and Hillel and the decrees of the earlier masters reflect economic and social conflict in Palestine (which we take up presently) is not supported by reference to archaeological or even extra-Talmudic literary evidence. Having postulated that economic issues were everywhere present, Ginzberg proceeded to use this postulate to "explain" a whole series of cases. The "explanations" are supposed to demonstrate the validity of the postulate, but in fact merely repeat and illustrate it.

What is lacking in each particular case is the demonstration that the data could not equally well -- or even better -- be explained by some other postulate or postulates. At best we are left with "this could have been the reason" but with no concrete evidence that this was the reason. Masses of material perhaps

---

[1]Even J. Wellhausen, *Die Pharisaer und die Sadducaer. Eine Untersuchung zur innerin judischen Geschichte* (Griefswald, 1874) seems to have known the rabbinic traditions about the Pharisees primarily through the medium of Derenbourg, *Essai* (below).

originally irrelevant are built into pseudo-historical structures which rest on nothing more solid than "we might suppose that." The deductive approach to the study of law ill serves the historian. One of the most common phrases in the historical literature before us is, "If this supposition is sound, then ..." I found it in nearly every historian who wrote in Hebrew. It is Talmudics extended to the study of history -- Talmudic history in a catastrophic sense.

I do not unreservedly condemn Talmudics, except in connection with historical studies. It is a great tradition, interesting and important as a phenomenon of intellectual history, beautiful and fascinating as an intellectual exercise, and a powerful instrument for apologetics and for the reinterpretation necessary to make ancient laws and doctrines apply to modern problems. I should not even deny that it may be a valuable instrument for philosophical research. For instance, Morton Smith comments on the work of Harry A. Wolfson, "Wolfson's achievements by his 'hypothetico-deductive method' are justly famous. But when Wolfson uses the method, the hypotheses are made from a minute study of the primary sources, and the deductions are checked at every point by careful consideration of the historical evidence, and those which cannot be confirmed are clearly indicated as conjectural." My objection is that when used by men without Wolfson's historical training, mastery, and conscience, the methods lends itself easily to abuse, to the invention of imaginary principles and distinctions for which there is no historical evidence whatsoever, and to the deduction of consequences which never appear in the texts. It can too easily be used to obscure real differences of opinion or practice, to explain away the evidences of historical change, and to produce a picture of antiquity which has no more similarity to the facts than the Judaism of contemporary New York does to that of ancient Palestine.

A further, even more serious impediment to the development of the historical study of Talmudic literature was the need for apologetics. Talmudists with university training encountered the anti-Pharisaic, anti-Judaic, and anti-Semitic attitudes (I cannot distinguish among these theological and racist species of a single genus of bigotry) of Christian scholars, who carried out polemical tasks of Christian theology in the guise of writing history. The Jewish historians undertook the defense. Two polemical themes recur.

First, the Christians' account of the Pharisees ignores rabbinic sources, therefore in incomplete. The reason is that the Christian scholars do not know the rabbinic literature, therefore whatever they say may be discounted because of their "ignorance."

Second, the Pharisees were the very opposite of what Christians say about them.

The former polemic produced the Christian response that the rabbinical materials are not reliable, because they are "late" or "tendentious." Many Christian scholars drew back from using rabbinic materials, or relied on what they presumed to be accurate, secondary accounts of them, because they were thoroughly intimidated by the claims of the Jewish opposition as to the difficulty of properly understanding the materials, and because they had slight opportunity to study the materials with knowledgeable scholars of Judaism. The latter polemic -- to prove the Pharisees the opposite of what had been said of them -- was all too successful. When Christian scholars became persuaded that the earlier Christian view had been incorrect, they took up the polemic in favor of the Pharisees. In doing so, they of course relied on Jewish scholarship and took over uncritically its uncritical attitude toward the material. Consequently, on both sides, sources were more often cited as facts than analyzed as problems. We commonly find a source cited without attention to how the citation is supposed to prove the "fact" it purportedly contains. Systematic analysis of texts is rare; allusion to unexamined texts is commonplace.

All previous studies of the rabbinic traditions about the Pharisees prove seriously inadequate, because, in general, the historical question is asked too quickly and answered uncritically. The inadequacy results from the false presumption that nearly all sources, appearing in any sort of document, early, late, or medieval, contain accurate historical information about the men and events of which they speak. The historians are further to be blamed for allowing the theologians to set the issue: Were the Pharisees really hypocrites? On the part of the Jewish scholars, the issues were, What shall we say in response to the Christian theological critique of Pharisaism? How shall we disprove the allegations of the Christians' holy books? On the Christian side, there were few "historians" worthy of the name, for most served the Church and not the cause of accurate and unbiased historical knowledge. Since the Christian theological scholars set the agenda, the Jewish ones can hardly be condemned for responding to it, especially since contemporary anti-Semitism was both expressed and aided by the Christian scholarly assessment of Pharisaism. In fact the European Jewish scholars turn out to have been fighting for the lives of the Jews of their own day and place. They lost that fight. It was a worthy effort, but it was not primarily an exercise of critical scholarship, and it seriously impeded the development of scholarly criticism.

The history of scholarship on the Pharisees thus cannot be divorced from the history of Judaism and of Christianity in the nineteenth and twentieth centuries, from the sociology of the Jews in Europe and the USA, and from the interrelationships between the two religious traditions. It is not our problem to describe the course of those complex and interrelated histories. We have instead to demonstrate in detail how those handicaps pointed out above -- anachronistic presuppositions, Talmudic method, and apologetic purpose -- have vitiated previous studies of the Pharisees. The reader may then measure those statements against the evidences he has already reviewed. He will observe two recurrent faults: first, the claim that a story contains an exact historical record of what actually happened; second, the tendency to say far more than all the data together permit. For the former error, evidence is not only abundant, but obvious. For the latter, the various generalizations about the Pharisees will have to be measured against the substance of the rabbinic traditions about Pharisees, upon which such gross generalizations largely rely. It might have been better to state the essential argument of each book or article, then to point out what is wrong with it. But to do so, I should have had to enter into the discussion of issues defined by historians to begin with not competent to formulate worthwhile issues for argument. I thereby should have implicitly suggested that the modern historiographical tradition had formulated arguable questions, and that its fundamental grasp of the evidence was sound. This is the opposite of the truth. I therefore cannot attempt to refute, point by point, statements which are made upon no foundation other than a false conception of the character of the evidence and of the nature of historical inquiry.

iv

Judeo-Christian Apologetics

R. Travers Herford, *The Pharisees* (repr. Boston, 1962), Leo Baeck, *The Pharisees and Other Essays* (N.Y., 1947), and George Foot Moore, *Judaism in the First Centuries of the Christian Era* (Vols. I-III, Cambridge, 1954) mark the high point of the apologetic movement. Hereford observes that the German and other non-Jewish scholars "all seem to have the contrast with Christianity more or less consciously present in their minds, not realizing that two things cannot be rightly compared until it has first been ascertained what each of them is in itself ... to call the New Testament as the chief witness upon the question who the Pharisees really were is false in logic and unsound in history." The Jewish scholars "know what Pharisaism is like from the inside" -- as if the rationalistic Judaism of the nineteenth century were still Pharisaism! Lauterbach is Hereford's guide: The Pharisees stood for the Oral Tradition. For his historical account, Hereford turns to Josephus (a prejudiced and unreliable source), whose story he embellishes with some Talmudic stories (mostly late second and third century A.D.). The descriptions of "Pharisaic religion" then draw upon the whole corpus of rabbinic literature.

G.H. Box seems to me to have been among the first to call attention to the development of apologetics in a Jewish counter-attack on Christian scholarship about the Pharisees. G.H. Box, "Survey of Recent Literature on the Pharisees and Sadducees," *Review of Theology and Philosophy* IV, 1908-9, pp. 129-151, discusses fourteen items published between 1900 and 1908, including encyclopedia articles, brief monographs, and major studies. What impressed Box was that "Jewish scholarship is beginning to assert itself in the domain of New Testament historical science." The issues defined by that scholarship centered upon the evaluation of the Pharisees: Were they all really hypocritical, or merely some of them? Was their legalism merely stiff and lifeless, dry and trivial, or was it sincere and inward?

The Jewish critique of Bousset and Schuerer (among others) began with the assertion that the non-Jewish scholars simply did not understand Pharisaic Judaism, because they did not control its sources. Had they understood rabbinic literature, they would have seen the Pharisees were "men of cultivated character and of piety true and deep." Only when Jewish scholars touched on New Testament materials did the Christians meet the attack. For reasons integral to his thesis about the extent of the purity laws, Buechler alleged that Mark 7:1ff. is "not authentic as an incident in the life of Jesus." Box then found it necessary to differ. One might say whatever he liked about the Pharisees. In the spirit of the early twentieth-century Anglo-American scholarship on the subject, favorable judgments on the Pharisees would be more readily accepted than unfavorable ones.

A second Jewish polemic had to do with the "guilt" for the trial and death of Jesus. Since Jesus had said and done nothing "which would render him liable to the death penalty according to the criminal law of the Pharisees (of which we have exact knowledge) [!], his death was the work of "the Sadducean High Priesthood." No one now claimed to inherit "Sadducean Judaism," and on the Jewish side, everyone purported to be true heirs of the Pharisees, so it seemed safe to blame the Sadducees. Box phrases the now-predominant issue: "One of the most difficult problems that confronts the New Testament student who wishes to take account of the Jewish background and to be just to the Palestinian Judaism of the first Christian century is concerned with the classification and estimate of the great Jewish parties, especially the Pharisees and Sadducees" (p. 132).

v

Critical Studies

From the late nineteenth century onward, a few historians have made intelligent use of Talmudic materials. They have avoided assuming that rabbinic texts always are accurate accounts of things that really happened. They have compared various versions of a story without supposing that every detail of every version contributes to a factual picture. They have used common sense. The pseudorthodox reading of the materials therefore had to compete with a dispassionate historical evaluation of sources, item by item. The tragedy of the field at hand derives from the failure of the generality of scholars to pay any attention to the excellent work that some carried on. Things did not have to turn out as they have. Let me cite only a few examples.

Israel Lévi, "Les sources talmudiques de l'histoire juive. I. Alexandre Jannée et Simon ben Schetah. II. La rupture de Jannée avec les Pharisiens," *REJ* 35, 1897, pp. 213-223, observes that many stories used by historians for the reconstruction of Pharisaic history are no more than *aggadot*, imaginary anecdotes for edification and amusement. This observation then is illustrated by the stories of Simeon, Jannaeus and the Nazirites. Levi compares the texts and notes the differences. He finds it incongruous that the Persian embassy wants nothing more than to hear wise teachings of the rabbi. The king is represented as naive. The whole is in the spirit of a fable: "It would not be difficult to uncover in medieval literature numerous parallels, not to mention equivalent fables in Midrashic literature, to which no one assigns historical value."

H. Stourdzé, "La fuite en Egypte de Josue b. Perahya et l'incident avec son pretendu disciple Jesus," *REJ* 82, 1926, pp. 133-156, appropriately appears in the festschrift to Israel Lévi. Stourdzé holds that the story of Joshua and Jesus has no historical value. He first reviews various discussions of the passage: Krochmal, Weiss, Frankel, Graetz, Yavetz, Halevy, and Hyman all regard the stories of Judah b. Tabbai and Joshua b. Perahiah as of historical value. For them Judah fled to Egypt, and later on, so did Joshua [!]. This he finds unlikely. The several hypotheses do not stand up under close examination. He compares the versions of the stories and finds the Palestinian Talmud's simpler and more 'natural.' The story is an imaginary anecdote, of no historical value whatever. Stourdze adds, "Mettre en doute la veracité d'une assertion est une idée modern. A l'époque talmudique, les parties discutaient, expliquaient, chacun d'apres ses principes, les affirmations de l'adversaire, mais ne le contestaient pas." Henceforward, therefore, Stourdzé's analysis is literary and tradition-critical, and not historical. I cannot imagine a more correct approach.

George Foot Moore, "Simeon the Righteous," *Jewish Studies in Memory of Israel Abrahams* (N.Y., 1927), pp. 348-364, alludes to the rabbinical stories, concluding only that Simeon "stands out in the memory of the age from which the legends come as the end of an epoch." He looks in second century A.D. problems for the animus of the stories of Meir and Judah about the Egyptian temple, treats the context in which the stories stand, and pays attention to the problem of QSQLGS and other materials. None of these pericopae serves Moore as the basis for his comments on the historical Simeon. At best, he argues, the "Simeon ... of the rabbinical sources" is to be put in the period located on the basis of other, more persuasive evidences. The Avot chain is examined. Moore sees that "at least one link is lacking," and thinks Antigonus of Sokho had students who were cut out. Moore's account of Simeon stands out. Unlike Schuerer, Moore both mastered and respected the Talmudic materials; like him, Moore read them in a critical spirit. I cannot explain why the examples of critical use of evidence derive from France and America, none from Germany, where in biblical studies work was so different.

vi

Traditional Studies

The scholars who worked within the received ("traditional") presuppositions about the divinely revealed character of the literature could not be expected to know better. But, interestingly, among the best work came from them. For knowing their own limitations, and also mastering the texts at hand in detail, they asked questions appropriate to their learning and avoided those inappropriate to the methods they found themselves constrained to use. The difference between the traditional and the pseudo-critical and pseudorthodox scholars lies in the simple absence of pretention characteristic of the former. Without doubt the most ambitious and impressive traditional historian of the rabbinic traditions about the Pharisees -- as of every other topic in "Talmudic history" -- is Y. I. Halevy. I call him 'traditional' because Halevy makes no pretense of approaching materials as a participant in the *wissenschaftliche* or scientific tradition. He enjoys destroying the results of those who do. But his thoroughness, profound knowledge of law, willingness to analyze texts in depth and to criticize all authorities, ancient and modern -- these mark Halevy as the greatest master of "Talmudic history" of his generation. Obviously, one cannot assent to his ridiculous conclusions. He regards as facts the allegations of the tradition as to its own history -- it begins at Sinai, or, least, before Ezra -- and of course takes for granted that what stories tell is what really happened, what laws prescribe is what actually was done. For him these are natural assumptions, but not impediments to the critical analysis of all problems. Citing his results would impede the exposition. It is important simply to record that the traditionalists among historians produced work of a critical order.[2]

vii

Pseudorthodox, Pseudocritical and Fundamentalist Studies

Halevy ridicules the misleading impression given by "the German sages" that they possess more accurate information than they actually have. What seems to me equally absurd is the gullible and uncritical use of Talmudic traditions, combined with the pretentious claim that, for the first time, something both new and "scientific" is being done with them. All of the studies we are about to consider take for granted what should be the problem, namely, the facticity or 'historicity' of the source. What is more, they merely allude to a pericope, without citing or analyzing it. We shall see the same use of sources in many of the contemporary continuators of gullibility. For example, one will find: "Hillel ousted the Bathyrans by citing his masters, Shema'iah and Abtalion," with an accompanying footnote, b. Pesahim 66b. We hear nothing of the several versions of the story, of how the author understands the introduction of new materials, the rearrangements of old, the inclusion of interpolations of various sorts (including the names of S + A), and so on. The readers will therefore assume that the historian has facts, and that the task is to interpret or explain facts. They will not see the frail foundations beneath such facts. In this regard, Lévi, Stourdzé, and Moore stand nearly by themselves.

---

[2]Yishaq Isaak Halevy, *Dorot HaRishonim* (German title: *Die Geschichte und Literatur Israels. Ic. Umfasst den Zeitraum von Ende der Hasmonäerzeit zur Einsetzung der römischen Landpfleger*, Berlin-Vienna, 1923), pp. 89-143, 547 ff.

Before proceeding, let us take up this neologism, *pseudorthodoxy*, which I have introduced here. It derives from Morton Smith, "The Present Stage of Old Testament Studies," *Journal of Biblical Literature* 88, 1969, pp. 19-35. Smith defines pseudorthodoxy as "the attempt to reconcile the traditional beliefs about the OT with the undeniable results of scholarship." Of greatest interest here are Smith's remarks about higher criticism, "which has always been the bete noire of the pseudorthodox. They were clever enough to see that its results had to be accepted. On the other hand, to attack higher criticism was the accepted way of vindicating pseudorthodoxy. Therefore higher criticism had to be both attacked and accepted. What could be done? The solution was: to concentrate the attack on the greatest and most famous representative of higher criticism, to announce to the public that his 'system' had been destroyed, and to appropriate privately its elements." Smith's pseudorthodox, and our pseudocritical, scholars have only the "pseudo" in common. The pseudocritical scholars claim to accept a critical approach, but in pretending that the sources are accurate historical records, and in failing to articulate and defend that notion, they reveal the fundamentalist convictions which they both hold and claim to transcend. They do not argue with the critical scholars. They either vilify or ignore them. Or the pseudocritical scholars will allege that they grant the presuppositions of the opposition, then completely bypass them, pretending nothing has changed. This we shall see in Chapter Four, in, for example, Cohen, Schiffman, and others. It comes down to the same thing. Ironically, we face the opposite of Smith's pseudorthodox: the pseudocritical scholars announce to the public that they are "critical" but privately they appropriate nothing whatever of the literary and historical-critical advances of the past century and a half of biblical studies.[3]

What commonly characterizes the pseudocritical school are some or all of these qualities:

first, deductive reasoning;

second, arbitrary and groundless judgments as to the historicity and the lack of historicity of various individual pericopae;

third, failure to bring to bear a wide range of evidence external to the Talmudic materials;

fourth, the assumption that whatever is alleged in any source is as well attested as what is alleged in any other;

fifth, the endless positing of untested, and untestable, possibilities;

sixth, the recurrent claim that a story "must have been supported by tradition";

seventh, the repeated argument that if a story were not true, no one would have told or preserved it;

---

[3]But Smith himself thinks that we can say a great deal about the "historical Jesus," and he picks and chooses which pieces of evidence he thinks provide the real facts. No one today trembles before his *Jesus the Magician*.

eighth, the spinning out of large theories to take account of stories and sayings under some grand philosophical scheme (which is not much different from the next);

ninth, a love of homiletics;

tenth, the invention of new definitions for old data, e.g., the use of proto-Pharisees, to describe the dim figures who link the Pharisees we know about to the alleged, earlier men of the Great Assembly about whom we know nothing;

eleventh and above all, what I find most telling is simple: *presumably, must* or *may have been* and *perhaps*, a few sentences later magically converted into *was* and *certainly,* -- these sleights of hand everywhere recur.

The pseudocritical scholars claim to write history, but the historicity of their histories is superficial, not profound. They concentrate on the exegesis of discrete pericopae. Further, as we shall see in Chapter Three below, they take up one rabbi after another in chronological order and describe as historical facts the stories and dicta attributed to him by any and all sources. They never get behind such sources to events or situations indicated by both but different from either.

How to proceed? While in my original survey, I took up as many theses on the Pharisees as I could find, in the present context a different procedure serves my purpose. I shall deal with only four prior approaches to the description, analysis, and interpretation of the Pharisees, all in English, all substantial figures in their day, and all interesting minds. For all of them presented theses worth debate, imaginative and suggestive propositions. Say what you will about their primitive conception of the problem of historical knowledge, none can deny the force of intellect in their enterprise. In this regard they tower over their continuators in gullibility, who carry forward the premise but not the intellect. We consider, then, representative theses of Ginzberg, Finkelstein, Zeitlin, and Lauterbach.

The single most famous work is Louis Ginzberg, "The Significance of the Halachah for Jewish History," *On Jewish Law and Lore* (Philadelphia, repr. 1962), pp. 77-126, who proposed "to demonstrate that the development of the halachah ... is not a creation of the House of Study but an expression of life itself." He proceeds to explain laws attributed to early authorities so as to illustrate that proposition. He turns, in particular, to a decree attributed to two early authorities that, first, cultic uncleanness applies to all land outside of the Land of Israel, and, second, articles made out of glass were susceptible to cultic uncleanness, by analogy that is to metal ones rather than to stone ones, which were not so susceptible. How then does Ginzberg explain these rulings?

The decree of the two Yosé's about the uncleanness of foreign countries and of glass was imposed "at the time when, as a result of the persecution by Antiochus Epiphanes, emigration from the Holy Land began. During that period contemporary leadership feared the threat of mass evacuation as a great danger to the nation and its land. Therefore, as a preventive measure, they ruled that foreign lands were impure." Ginzberg claims that glass was very expensive, though it seems to have been cheap. Many preferred glass vessels, "which could not become ritually impure, to locally produced earthenware and metal dishes, which required safeguarding against ritual impurity ... When ritual impurity was decreed for glassware this competition was partially lessened, since glassware from Tyre and Sidon no longer possessed the advantage of being free from the liability to ritual impurity" -- as if the masses kept the purity-laws!

Ginzberg takes up a decree attributed to another early figure, that cultic uncleanness affects wheat deriving from Alexandria. He says, "It is ... well known that the competition between the Holy Land and Egypt in the grain trade, and particularly in wheat, was very great indeed; when, consequently, Joshua ben Parahya became aware that some apprehension of impurity existed with respect to Alexandrian wheat, he used it as the reason for a restrictive decree intended for the benefit of Jewish farmers. He hoped that the majority of buyers would prefer the wheat of the Holy Land, which was not conditioned to receive impurity, to impure foreign wheat. His colleagues ... disagreed, for they preferred for the sake of the general good to encourage competition in foodstuffs."

Let me proceed rapidly to survey other propositions along these same lines. Simeon b. Shetah's decree on metal vessels came because "people began to import into the Holy Land other metals ... In order to protect native products, the susceptibility to ritual impurity was also decreed on these foreign metals, lest they be preferred to the metals of the Holy Land ..." To be sure, Palestine had no metals to speak of. Before the Houses, "it is established ... that there were not many conflicts of opinion among the sags of Israel." The differences between the Houses cannot be systematized. Many factors caused them. Shammai and Hillel did not found the Houses; they date back to the beginning of the pairs. But then from the beginnings there were many conflicts of opinion, or Ginzberg contradicts himself.

The Pharisees were split into two wings, right and left, conservatives and progressives. The controversy about laying on of hands "stems from the differences between the conservatives and the progressives." "It is my view that the conflict among the Pairs was over the issue whether obligatory burnt-offerings and obligatory peace-offerings required the laying on of hands, for the Torah mentions the laying on of hands only in connection with votive burnt-offerings and votive peace-offerings or in the cases of a guilt-offering or sin-offering." The controversy involved four questions.

1. The extent to which scholars were empowered to derive new enactments by means of biblical exegesis: The conservatives wanted to limit the authority of biblical exegesis as a source of new law. Therefore laying on of hands was not required, since the Bible does not mention it.

2. The participation of the public, not merely priests, in the Temple service: The progressives favored increasing the influence of the people on the Temple, therefore said the people may lay on hands.

3. Use of laying on of hands as a means of increasing the return of the Jews to the Holy Land: The progressives wished to use the ritual as propaganda towards that end.

4. Equality between Jews of the Holy Land and those of the diaspora in offering their sacrifices: The conservatives said it was sufficient for the Jews to send obligatory burnt-offerings. The progressives said in favor of the diaspora that there is no distinction between votive and obligatory burnt-offerings; in both instances laying on of hands is required.

As to the differences between the Houses, "the usual interpretation is that these two Schools expressed the personalities of their founders, the conciliatory Hillel and the unyielding Shammai." But this is not so. The real difference goes back before the two masters; the differences were over social and economic policy. For example, Ginzberg cites M. Ber. 6:5, "If one pronounces a benediction over the bread, he need not recite one over the side-dishes ..." "The reason for the disagreement was that bread was the main dish of the poor man's meal, and, therefore, once he recited a benediction over the bread, he thereby blessed the entire meal; for the rich man, however, who ate meat, fish, and all kinds of delicacies, bread was not the main dish. The school of Shammai ... maintained that even cooked foods were not included in a benediction over bread." Other differences concerning the meal were "based on the class difference between the Schools."

Further, slaughtering a wild animal or bird on a festival day (M. Bes. 1:1) produces a disagreement resulting "from the class differences between the two Schools. The eating of game or birds was quite usual for the rich but not for the poor ..." As to the several cases in which the Houses differ on the matter of intention: "Primitive man reckoned only with the act, and not with the intention; a man was judged by his deeds and not by his thoughts ... We therefore find the School of Shammai, the representatives of the conservatives, considered deed more important than thought. In many cases involving laws of things prohibited and permitted ... they declared that deed is paramount, as over against the progressive view of the School of Hillel, who taught that an act not accompanied by intention is not to be considered an act."

Now what do I find wrong with all this? Ginzberg's picture depends upon the presupposition, not only that the decrees were made by those to whom they were attributed, but also that they were enforced. The Pharisees were in control of the government. Whatever they decreed had the force of law. The Hasmoneans were subservient to their wishes even at the very outset of their rule (the Yosi's). The decrees of the Yosé's were confirmed by the monarch, who presumably "sat humbly" before the Pharisaic masters. The government was, moreover, both sophisticated in matters of economics, and also able to carry out sweeping decrees pretty much as the Pharisaic masters issued them. One could argue in Ginzberg's behalf that the Pharisees might have decided their legal questions by considerations of public interest even though they knew their decisions would produce no practical consequences. If the presupposition that the law made by Pharisees was enforced was false, that fact would not render the rest of the structure impossible. What is weak is that Ginzberg never raises the question of whether and how the Pharisees enforced their rulings.

Ginzberg must have taken for granted the historicity of all the laws: they were made by those to whom they were attributed, and they were kept by everyone else. He does not bring a shred of evidence to substantiate any of his theories, e.g., that there was emigration at the time of the Maccabees, that everyone kept the purity laws, that many preferred glass vessels, that Joshua had the power and knowledge to help out the farmers, and that they needed help; that people began to import other metals in the time of Simeon b. Shetah, and that he had the power to prevent it. The Houses' disputes go back a century and a half before the establishment of the Houses, even though we have no hint of that fact in the sources attributed to antecedent authorities. The Pharisees were split into conservatives and progressives; so too the Sadducees were conservative and the Pharisees progressive, and so on. Wherever we find two parties, the difference between them will be explained in the same way. The explanation is not accompanied by archeological or historical facts. Everything is argued on the basis of what sounds reasonable. So the argument from content is not an invention of today's generation.

Student and disciple of Ginzberg, Louis Finkelstein carried forward the same theory of the nature and use of the Talmudic evidence. This he did in, e.g., *HaPerushim ve Anshe Keneset HaGedolah* (N.Y., 1950: *The Pharisees and the Man of the Great Synagogue)* and *The Pharisees. The Sociological Background of Their Faith* (Philadelphia, 1962). He treats as fact the economic-sociological thesis of Ginzberg. For him the plebeians are urban workers, against the rural gentry. Differences in wealth were secondary. The Houses did not debate old vs. new law. The real differences were between provincials and metropolitans; they reflected differences of habitat. The struggle was "carried on in Palestine for fifteen [!] centuries." For example, the Hillelites were sympathetic to the Judean grape-growers; the "patrician Shammaites" favored the Galilean olive-producers -- accounting for the difference of opinion between the masters recorded in b. Shab. 17a. Likewise, Shema'iah, a plebeian, believed in the merit of the fathers. The patricians denied pre-determination." "Abtalyon, the patrician, maintains that the miracle was caused by the merit of the Israelites themselves." In his *Akiba, Scholar, Saint and Martyr* (Philadelphia, repr. 1962), he again has the Shammaites as patricians, the Hillelites as plebeians. Simeon b. Gamaliel "scion of the House of Hillel" defected to the Shammaites: "Social position meant everything to Simeon ben Gamaliel, and he could not bear to risk its loss. His abandonment of the Hillelite School was not merely formal and outward; it was inner and complete. He had inherited the mind of his ancestors, but not their spirit, their shrewdness but not their understanding, their keen insight but not their broad sympathies and social conscience ... Above all, he had lost that fundamental quality of self-effacement, which had made the House of Hillel universally revered. He could never forget himself. Vain, pompous, and egotistical, conscious of scholarly inferiority among the Hillelites and of social inferiority among the Shammaites, he found his greatest delight in dramatic exhibitions of personal authority." "Everything that Simeon ben Gamaliel did reflected his social ambitions. He lived in a fashionable court, where his nearest neighbor was a Sadducee." Finkelstein's tirade against the hapless Simeon b. Gamaliel represents the pseudocritical school's homiletics. The readers may refer to the little corpus of Simeon-materials which I published in my *Rabbinic Traditions about the Pharisees before 70, vol. I* to see whether they can find out what so irritated Finkelstein. I cannot account for his lengthy, hostile judgment.

We come now to Solomon Zeitlin. Certainly in his day a proponent of the highest standards of critical learning, in the historical area Zeitlin recapitulates the abysmal gullibility of his age. Zeitlin's papers confidently and repeatedly present as fact a wide range of quite dubious notions. But all of them rest on a single premise: the historicity of sayings and stories in the talmudic canon. For example, S. Zeitlin, "Prosbol, A Study of Tannaitic Jurisprudence," *Jewish Quarterly Review* 37, 1947, pp. 341-362, takes for granted the literal, historical accuracy of the *prosbol*-stories. He does not analyze the literary traits of the stories and sees no historical problems in them. The primary issue is legal, but what the law describes is taken for granted a social and historical fact. Elsewhere in Zeitlin's legal studies that premise makes slight difference to Zeitlin's analysis and thesis. Here, however, that assumption is central to the argument. Zeitlin claims, "Before his [Hillel's] time, the creditor in order not to lose the money which he had loaned to his fellow men on account of the sabbatical year, deposited with the court a promissory note given to him by the debtor. Such a promissory note had a clause to the effect that the real property of the debtor was mortgaged to the creditor. In such a case, the creditor had the right to collect the debt even after the sabbatical year ... According to the opinion of the school of Shammai, anything which ultimately has to be collected is considered as already collected [his footnote: *"b. Git. 37a"* -- which contains only a later interpretation]. However, that was only a custom and had not as yet been sanctioned. Hillel introduced the Takkana that the creditor may write a Prosbol, even without the knowledge of the debtor, in which he declares that he will collect all the debts people owe him. The Prosbol is valid, whether or not the creditor has a promissory note, and whether or not the note was deposited with the court. This Takkana Hillel made a law by supporting it by a verse in the Pentateuch. A Takkana must always be based on the Pentateuch."[4] Zeitlin thus

---

[4]I call attention to the very common assumption of the scholars at hand that all readers are Jewish and knowledgeable in the sources. Zeitlin clearly does not think he has to explain any of the technical terms at hand. He is not writing for an audience beyond the limits of the Yeshiva-world. We shall see the same rather limited vision in the writing of Cohen and Schiffman, among others. They are talking to people who know, pretty much, what they are talking about to begin with -- the same sources, read in the same way. The contrast to Finkelstein should not be missed. He really expected to address a very large world and wrote for that world -- as any scholar does.

takes for granted that the Sabbatical laws were everywhere enforced. It was moreover possible for the Pharisees to effect changes in the administration of commercial (and real estate) law. Further, Zeitlin claims that the Prosbol was in existence before Hillel's time, which is not what the story says. He claims this was merely a "custom," but the story ways Hillel introduced that custom. Zeitlin has imposed a theory upon stories which in their present form contradict his theory. It hardly serves to argue that Hillel "really" did introduce the Prosbol as the stories say, against the view that all he did was to find a Scriptural basis for a rather minor alteration of existing practice. Indeed, one can hardly argue with this sort of allegation, without being drawn into the conceptually primitive framework of discussion. What Hillel "really" did or did not do is not a suitable subject for analysis, given the condition of the sources. Zeitlin thus intuits various sorts of novellae, offering his own certainty of the truth of his allegation in place of evidence or careful argumentation. Perhaps the most striking example of his quite arbitrary definitions is "The Semikah Controversy between the Zugoth," *JQR* 7, 1916-1917, pp. 499-517. Here Zeitlin proposes that the "lay-on-hands" of M. Hag. 2:2 has nothing to do with performing the ceremony of laying of hands upon the head of the sacrificial animal in the Temple-court on holidays. I shall spare the reader the details of the matter. But a more immediately accessible example of his capacity to read into the sources pretty much anything he wants is at hand. Zeitlin interprets the language of Shammai to Hillel in b. Shab. 17a, *"If you anger me..."* as follows: "If you will bring the principle of intention to prevail, I shall decree that olives are also made susceptible to levitical uncleanness by their own liquid though no one desires this superfluity." This is made up by Zeitlin, a kind of learned homily. If it sounds right, it must be right.

Let me conclude our visit to Zeitlin with one final point. A characteristic of pseudocriticism is the resort to facile emendations to solve historical problems. Since the facticity of the historical stories is taken for granted, emending the sources will supply the answer to any difficulty and forthwith create a new fact. In his "Sameias and Pollion," *Journal of Jewish Lore and Philosophy* 1, 1919, pp. 61-67, Zeitlin reviews the references of Josephus and then asks, "Who are the two men ...?" He forthwith reviews various suggestions and possibilities, rejecting each in turn. In the end he concludes the references of Josephus are not always to the same men. In one passage Sameias is Shammai; in two others, he is Shemaiah. The consequences of this theory are then spelled out. Throughout, of course, the passages are treated as literally true and accurate accounts of what was really said and done. Zeitlin then turns to Pollion the Pharisee. He concludes that this figure must be Hillel. But Zeitlin recognizes that we have another figure by the same name, namely, Josephus's Pollion, who is represented as teacher of Sameias. Here is how Zeitlin solves this problem: "But Hillel was not the teacher of Shemaiah -- he was his pupil. This reversing of relations can be explained as due to a scribal error."

Like Louis Ginzberg, Jacob Z. Lauterbach enjoyed wide influence for several decades. Hereford says that he revised his own views of the Pharisees after reading Lauterbach. Lauterbach posits his own set of theories to account for various disputes. In general, he falls in line with the opinion of Reform Jewish scholars, beginning with Geiger, that the Sadducees were reactionaries, the Pharisees liberals. The whole then is embellished with sermons of various kinds. The sources invariably supply facts, and the scholar then interprets these facts. The starting point is the fact.

In his papers, "The Sadducees and Pharisee," "A Significant Controversy between the Sadducees and the Pharisees," and "The Pharisees and their Teachings," *Rabbinic Essays* (Cincinnati, 1951, pp. 23-50, 51-86, 87-162, respectively, Lauterbach postulates that the Sadducees were the older, more conservative party, the Pharisees the younger, "broader and more liberal in their views, of progressive tendencies and not averse to innovations." Lauterbach treats the division of the two parties, which he assigns to early (!) in Second Temple times. Pharisees emerge from lay teachers, the Sadducees were formed by the priestly aristocracy. Like Moore, Lauterbach draws upon the whole corpus of rabbinic literature for his description of the Pharisees (called "sages of Israel"). The upshot for Lauterbach? He finds antecedents for Reform Judaism, specifically: the Pharisees claimed the right to make laws necessary for their time. The Sadducees denied that right. "Sadducaism because of its rigid conservatism in following the letter of the Law, gradually lost all influence upon the life of the main body of the Jewish people."

The significant controversy between the parties concerned the manner in which the high priest should bring in the incense into the Holy of Holies on the Day of Atonement. "The Sadducees said it must be prepared outside of the Holy of Holies. The Pharisees said it should not be put into the censer outside, but the high priest should enter the Holy of Holies carrying the censer with the fiery coals in his right hand and the spoon full of incense in this left hand. Only inside the curtain should he put the incense upon the fiery coals on the censer and thus offer it there." Lauterbach asks how the Pharisees could have known the law, when the Sadducees were in control of the Temple. The Pharisees, he claims to prove, introduced "a radical reform." The Sadducees retained "many of the primitive notions both about God and the purpose of the service offered to Him in the Temple." The Pharisees had a "purer God conception and less regard for the sacrificial cult ... They tried ... to democratize and spiritualize the service in the Temple and to remove from it ... the elements of crude superstition and primitive outworn conceptions." Preparing the incense outside was a measure of precaution; the smoke would protect the priest from "the danger of Satan's accusations ..." Further, the smoke would prevent the high priest from "involuntarily looking the Deity in the face ..." These "primitive theological views" were rejected by the Pharisees.

"The Pharisees and their Teachings" makes the same point, that the Pharisees offered a "more spiritual" conception of religion than did their opposition. Their victory "had to result in a broad liberal universalism." Christianity sprang from Pharisaic Judaism. "Jesus and his disciples did not belong to the priestly aristocratic party of the Sadducees. They were of the plain humble people who followed the Pharisees." Each of the ancient sources, the Talmud, Josephus, and the New Testament, preserves "some accurate information about these two parties." The Pharisees were the newer party, the Sadducees the older; they were conservative, strict interpreters of the Torah. The Pharisees were "the younger, progressive party composed originally of democratic laymen who outgrew some of the older notions, cherished modern and liberal ideas, and therefore became separated from the older group and formed a distinct party. They were the liberal separatists, the dissenters who rejected some of the ancient traditional conceptions of religion and who broke away the primitive traditional attitude toward the Torah ..." All of this obviously serves the cause of the theology of Reform Judaism.

Before concluding, let me beg the reader's indulgence for one final case, that of Armand Kaminka, who exhibits a commendable skepticism about some materials, but thorough-going gullibility about others. I introduce him because he embodies the wonderful simplicity of the entire school at hand. For one thing, if everyone thinks *this*, Kaminka (like many he represents) announces that the fact, in fact, is *that*. If up, then down, if black, then white. The traditional talmudic *hiddush* (novella) often involved the claim that what everyone took for granted was false, but the very opposite was true. In Kaminka's case, this meant turning Hillel from a Babylonian into an Alexandrian -- "perhaps" a provincial judge from Jericho (!). His sayings can be set at particular historical times and made to refer to particular events. So behind the facade of skepticism lies the usual pseudocritical attitude. In "Hillel's Life and Work," JQR 30, 1939-40, pp. 107-122, Kaminka recognizes that some of the Hillel-materials are unhistorical. Any priest in Jerusalem "could have testified with certainty as to how the ritual of the Passover sacrifice had been performed through long generations when the 14th day of Nisan fell on a Sabbath." The stories are spun out of "public addresses containing fables with ethical conclusions." The rise-to-power-story proves a haughty man loses his wisdom. The story of Hillel's hardships shows "poverty is no excuse for neglecting the study of the Law." Other materials likewise are for didactic purposes and should not be treated as historical. It is unlikely that Hillel, a poor man from abroad, "should have been suddenly chosen for a high position." All this testifies that Kaminka asked critical questions. But what then follows? The office of nasi did not exist. Hillel came from Alexandria, not Babylonia; this is shown by the story of Hillel's ruling in the Alexandrian marriage-contract case. Hillel was born about 75 B.C.E. Shammai's saying (b. Qid. 43a) that one who tells someone to kill is guilty of murder explains how the judges acquitted Herod: A murderer is only the one who actually sheds blood, and "Shammai" opposed the ruling. He is the

Sameias mentioned by Josephus. Hillel's saying, "A name made great is a name destroyed," and "Those that drowned you will be drowned" refer to great historical events, e.g., the battle of Pharsalus (48 B.C.E.). Hillel's saying alluded in fact to Pompey, and "it is to the skull of the latter that he addressed the verse ..." (!). A. Kaminka, "Hillel and his Works," in Hebrew, Zion 4, 1939, pp. 258-266 (= JQR 30,107-122) says Hillel came from Alexandria and had been "perhaps a judge in Jericho when this city was under the rule of Cleopatra." Pollion was Hillel. Again, the story about the skull floating on the water "was told about Pompey who drowned near Alexandria after the battle of Pharsalus." All of this is simply made up for the occasion.

Enough said.

viii

Anti-Semitic Theology in Historical Guise

If I have neglected accounts of Pharisaism by non-Jewish scholars, the reason is that most are beneath criticism. What they lack are concern to portray the Pharisees accurately and dispassionately and willingness to abandon theological interests in favor of historical ones. To take only one example among innumerable candidates, Protestant and Catholic alike, Reginald H. Fuller writes (in *The Book of the Acts of God. Contemporary Scholarship Interprets the Bible*, by G. Ernest Wright and Reginald H. Fuller [N.Y., 1960], pp. 229-231),

> "The dominant concern of the Pharisaic movement was to preserve inviolate the Mosaic law and its way of life against the encroachments of alien cultures. Since that law had been given once for all through Moses there could be no new laws. Instead, the ancient laws, which had been intended for a more primitive society, had to be reapplied to later situations. In this reapplication there was no thought of introducing novelties: rather, the idea was to extract the real meaning of the law."

In the rabbinic traditions about the Pharisees, one will look in vain for the articulate expression of Fuller's "dominant concern." As to not making new laws, Fuller seems not to have noticed the later rabbinic interpretations of the authority of ad hoc rulings made by sages (*taqqanot*). As the Jewish scholars repeatedly claim, considerable efforts were made to change the law, and not merely through reinterpretation or causistry. Further, he reveals a theological bias:

> "There was little attempt to search for an underlying principle behind the numerous commands and prohibitions. The two great commandments, love of God and love of the neighbor, were of course part of the law, but even in combination they were not accorded that central and unifying position which they were given in the New Testament. All this naturally led to legalism and

scrupulosity, to a belief in the saving value of good works, and the consequent sense of pride which a doctrine of merit inevitably entailed."

Countless stories make precisely the point Fuller denies was central in the Pharisaic tradition. To Hillel, just as to Jesus, is given the saying that Lev. 19:18 was "the whole Torah," thus surely "central" and "unifying." (To be sure Hillel may never have said any such thing, but such critical considerations do not enter Fuller's argument.) Fuller thus misrepresents the Pharisaic position, and one must ask why. The answer follows in his next sentence. The references to legalism and scrupulosity and the saving value of good works tells us that Fuller judges Pharisaic Judaism by the theology of classical Christianity. Legalism is a bad thing; belief in the saving value of good works obviously is inferior to "faith." The theological bias natural to a Christian theologian has prevented Fuller from carefully examining the Pharisaic literature and accurately representing what he finds there.

What is wrong with the Pharisees is that they were not Christians. Therefore one may do with the evidence anything he likes. For example, Fuller writes, "Hellenistic Judaism became a missionary religion. The statement in Matthew 23:15: '... you traverse sea and land to make a single proselyte ...' may be an exaggeration, as far as Palestine is concerned, but it was certainly true of the dispersion." Fuller carefully omits the opening part of the saying: "woe unto you, Scribes and Pharisees." For Fuller the verse therefore testifies about "Hellenistic Judaism," of which it does not speak, and not about Pharisaic Judaism, to which it explicitly refers. This sort of "revision" of evidence may suit theological purposes.

Fuller's account of the Pharisees is brief and plays no important role in his picture of early Christianity. I use it to exemplify traits which occur in grosser form in other works of the same origin. What it shows is that the large number of Christian scholars of Pharisaism, even in very recent times, first, do not see differences between theology and history and, second, do not take the trouble to examine the rabbinic evidences, either accepting or rejecting the whole without careful, thorough study. Of these faults, the second seems from a scholarly viewpoint the more damning. But when I originally published this critique and naively assumed he would take the occasion to reply, I waited in vain for his answer. He had nothing to say in his own behalf. "Silence is assent."

ix

Summary

First, we observe that few students of Pharisaism or of the rabbinic traditions about the Pharisees have thoroughly examined all pertinent sources. Second, a consistently critical, truly historical approach characterizes only a small number of scholars. What makes scholars pseudocritical, third, is the claim that they follow the normal canons of historical inquiry while at the same time they advances arguments alien to that inquiry; or that he credulously take as fact allegations contained in literature not actually analyzed. There is, further, the tendency to ignore the conceptual and methodological achievements of other scholars, both in the field of Talmudic studies and in cognate areas of inquiry. We look in vain, fourth, for the awareness that scholarship reflects the scholar's own sociological and historical situation. But the main problem is the one that persists: gullibility.

Chapter Three

The Case Of Biography
Eliezer Ben Hyrcanus

i
Introduction

We proceed from the use of evidence for describing a social group to use of the same evidence for biography. For that purpose I return to Eliezer ben Hyrcanus, on whom I did my last full-scale biographical study. It was at that point that I concluded biography was not a possibility. I note that, after my *Eliezer ben Hyrcanus. The Tradition and the Man* (Leiden, 1973: E. J. Brill) I-II, to my knowledge not a single book-length scholarly biography of a talmudic figure has appeared in Hebrew, German, French, or English. Whether the fundamentalists have given up the idea of lives of rabbis, or whether they have not got the energy and ambition to write them, I cannot say. But for fifteen years, we have seen none.

We now survey the use of evidence in the study of Eliezer. Not surprisingly, accounts of the life of Eliezer have in common a wholly uncritical approach to the sources.

First, while the problem of which Eliezer is referred to in various pericopae is raised, it is rarely systematically dealt with. Nearly everything attributed to any Eliezer is normally assumed to derive from ours in virtually every scholarly account before us.

Second, it is always taken for granted that whatever is attributed to Eliezer is what he actually said. Stories about him, moreover, relate what really happened. In the main, scholarship takes everything at face value. Scholars make composites of various tales into a single coherent narrative and organize the legal materials around a few basic issues -- e.g., Eliezer as conservative or as a Shammaite or as a patrician or as a logician. Efforts to examine the traditions about Eliezer add up to little more than compilations of those traditions, distinguished from one another by the episodic insertion of friendly or hostile homilies. While the earlier students of Eliezer take for granted the equal historical veracity of pretty much everything they find in all sources, early, late, and medieval, they do tend to select what they like and omit what they do not.[1]

In the main earlier accounts of Eliezer tend to ignore the legal materials, which permit a considerable study of Eliezer as a historical figure, in favor of those which purport to reveal his biography or philosophy. These have been strung together, according to the natural requirements of biography, into stories about his origins, education, active life, excommunication, melancholy old age, and his death. Were we to accept the biographical agendum, we should have to formulate ad hoc arguments about what is, and what is not, credible in the various legends about Eliezer told for many centuries after his life. Such arguments would constitute nothing more than the objectivization of intuitions. In the absence of solid evidence one can do little more than posit "reasons" for believing or disbelieving, in detail or in general, materials which to begin with exhibit no close connections to the historical character they claim to describe.

ii.

Compilations of Stories and Sayings

Biographies commonly consist in paraphrase of sayings and stories. The reader will not find interesting an endless paraphrase of such paraphrase. Let me therefore cite only one, the best known. Often cited because it originally appeared in German (I read it in Hebrew), Benjamin Zeev [Wilhelm] Bacher, *Aggadot HaTannaim* (Hebrew: A.Z. Rabinovitz) (Berlin, 1922), Vol. I, part i, pp. 72-114, surveys the non-legal pericopae, citing them in full, with brief notes. The substance of his paraphrase is as follows. Eliezer was one of the great disciples of the House of Hillel, but his harsh principles and conservative tendencies made him appear to be a Shammaite. The tradition, particularly stories, preserve his exact words as spoken in real life. It shows a very sharp mode of self-expression. He was exact in memorizing and preserving the teachings of his masters. He saw the destruction of the Temple as the beginning of a spiritual decline for Israel. He did not like proselytes. His tendency in the interpretation of Scripture was to exaggerate the miracles in those stories, e.g., two hundred plagues against the Egyptians at the sea. He stressed the importance of Sabbath rest, which was the main expression of the Covenant. He likewise laid special importance to honoring one's father and mother. He is not credited with knowledge of mystical sciences, but post-Talmudic literature attributed to him various mystical texts. What Bacher supplies is simply a *diatesseron* or, in simpler language, an academic pudding: everything harmonized into one thing.

---

[1]For instance, the matter of the excommunication of Eliezer and his involvement with minim is apt to be bypassed or dealt with in a cursory manner. Only a few have admitted their selectivity; none has justified it. We shall see the same trait in the contemporaries.

iii
Special Studies

Ben Zion Bokser and Louis Finkelstein provided more than routine paraphrases of sayings and stories on Eliezer. The former wrote an entire book, and the latter in works we have already noted made important and suggestive remarks. Both therefore provide us with a more than routine introduction to the regnant theory of the use of evidence for biographical purposes. Let me briefly review Bokser's findings, in his *Pharisaic Judaism in Transition. R. Eliezer the Great and Jewish Reconstruction after the War with Rome* (N.Y., 1935). He sees Eliezer (p. 5) as "a member of the upper class, a landed aristocrat...rigidly conservative in his conception of Jewish piety, social doctrine, and the champion of a static jurisprudence." He was repudiated as were the conservative Shammaites. He defied the majority and so was excommunicated. All this simply takes as fact a wide variety of tales, that occur in documents spread over nearly half a millenium.

The usual paraphrase of these stories follows: Eliezer studied with Yohanan despite his father's protests. The story of his origins proves Eliezer came from a family of landowners, began his studies as a mature man, and studied with Yohanan. Yohanan himself testifies to Eliezer's good memory. Eliezer was a great linguist and certainly was familiar with Greek. He was informed on subjects of a scientific nature. Eliezer was deeply attached to Yohanan. He was a Levite. He married Imma Shalom, Gamaliel's sister. His children were famous for their beauty. He also married his minor niece at his mother's insistence. He was wealthy and owned much land. He lived in Lydda, a town "particularly popular with the emigré aristocracy." During the anti-Christian persecutions, he was arrested on suspicion of heresy. Some see the reference to Jesus in the question about "a certain one" and his place in the world to come, b. Yoma 66b. But this is unsupported. It could as well be an allusion to Solomon.

Eliezer participated in the Yavnean school and also conducted his own. Aqiba began his career with Eliezer and Joshua. Eliezer also instructed Ilai, Nathan, Joseph b. Perida, Yosi, Abba Hanin, Yohanan b. Nuri, Judah b. Batyra, Haninah, and Judah b. Gaddish. Eliezer also collected funds for the rabbis, proclaimed fast days, and went to Rome with Gamaliel. This was in 116-117, in connection with the war against Trajan; the rabbis went to prevent retaliation. At his death people lamented that a scroll of the law had been destroyed.

He had unpolished manners, was crude of speech, and engaged in "bullying at the slightest provocation." When Yohanan's son died, he told him to have another one. He told Aqiba he would be slaughtered. He praised himself. He was a Shammaite and a dissenter at Yavneh. While he was a disciple of "an ardent Hillelite, R. Yohanan b. Zakkai," he also was a wealthy landowner and insisted on the status quo. At first his views were "repudiated as Shammaitic." But there was an open break on account of the oven of Akhnai. The opposition did not want the priests to evade the laws of Levitical uncleanness and objected to his ruling that the stove was clean. It was not broken, for the owner intended to continue to use it. The intention thus put it into the category of a whole vessel. Eliezer was more friendly to the priests and regarded the stove as actually broken. The rabbis not only excommunicated him but also burned all the types of priestly food he had regarded as ritually pure. He was in Rome in 117-118, so must have died thereafter, in Caesarea.

Eliezer opposed individualism and universalism in theology, defending the "more conservative" viewpoint. Likewise in matters of social doctrine: "His colleagues endeavored to continue the development in the direction of individualism and universalism, to reach out after a greater measure of social equality, a more thorough-going pacifism, and a more inclusive humanitarianism. He...dissented, representing the more conservative point of view." Similarly, his colleagues represented the forces of social change. They facilitated change and emphasized individualism. Eliezer opposed change and defended the status quo, emphasizing uniformity and stability: "The law is to him a great impersonal fact, a body of eternal and immutable formulae. The applications of the law are mechanical, in accordance with the dictates of a rigorous logic. Conditions under which the law has to be carried out are disregarded. Individualization is minimized." The conclusion is as follows:

> R. Eliezer was the disciple of an ardent Hillelite...He apparently accepted the formal repudiation of Shammaitism. But we know that he was a great landowner, a member of the upper class. It was consequently inevitable that, wherever Pharisaism was still flexible, he reasserts the point of view related to his class interests -- the old point of view of the Sadducees and the Shammaites. It was the common rural background which made him, like the Sadducees, 'boorish in behavior'...It was fully in consonance with his class traditions that he taught a theology in which there was very little concern for the individual; that he was hostile to the non-Jewish world and unfriendly to proselytizing propaganda; that he emphasized the Temple, the cult of sacrifices, and the priesthood; that he championed the interests of agriculture and defended the rights of property; that he was unsympathetic to the women, the poor, the lowly born, the slave, and the criminal. Conservative in his attitude toward piety and social doctrine, he like the Sadducees and the Shammaites was very naturally moved to develop a system of jurisprudence which emphasized stability, uniformity, and opposed change. That, like the Sadducees and the Shammaites, R. Eliezer too was finally repudiated is only an indication of the extent and the direction of the class struggle -- a struggle of which the combatants may not have been fully conscious, but which every utterance of theirs betrays.

So Bokser. It is what we get when we take it all as face-value.

Louis Finkelstein treats Eliezer in his works devoted to other subjects. But in his *Aqiba. Scholar, Saint, and Martyr* (Philadelphia, 1936; repr. 1962), he presents a discussion particularly suggestive of the mentality at hand. It involves disputes on the question of whether certain liquids impart susceptibility to uncleanness, in line with Lev. 11:34. In the context at hand, some do, some do not. Eliezer participated in a dispute on that matter -- so a source maintains. Now, as to the ritual status of liquids, Finkelstein writes as follows (pp. 97-100):

The interest of the patricians in the cultivation of olives, which had led to one of Aqiba's earliest controversies with Tarfon, formed the basis of an even more prolonged and bitter discussion with Eliezer. Since the olive had become the fruit par excellence of Galilee, the production of its oil in the prescribed "purity" involved serious difficulties. Living at a distance from Jerusalem and the Temple, the Galileans could hardly arrange to "cleanse" themselves when they became defiled by contact with the dead, for that particular form of "impurity" could be removed only with the ashes of the red heifer which were kept in the sanctuary (Num. 19:1ff). The Galileans, apparently, did bathe to wash away minor impurities, but in the eyes of the scholars this did not mitigate the effects of the major impurity. Legally they were "impure" and their touch contaminated. What, then, was to be done about the olives which they garnered? The Shammaites, who were especially concerned with this question, had an easy solution. They pointed to the verse in Leviticus (11:34) which denies that food can become impure unless it is moistened. The plucked olives were moist only with their own juice and, said the Shammaites, that liquid is not sufficient to render them susceptible to impurity. The Hillelites asked why the juice of grapes and all other fruits should be considered "preparation" for defilement and not the juice of olives. No satisfactory answer was given to this question, but the Shammaites insisted on their position.

This convenient rule did not, however, solve the whole problem. What was the status of the oil derived from the olives? The question was not merely academic and theoretical; nor did it concern only the super-pious who observed the laws of purity after the Temple was destroyed. It has a very practical importance, and involved vast property interests. The Heave-offering which every Jewish farmer in Palestine gave to the priest could be eaten only if it was pure. Obviously, if it was held that most of the olive oil produced in Galilee was impure, the priests would lose a large fraction of their income.

The situation was aggravated rather than mitigated by the destruction of the Temple. While the ashes of the last red heifer had somehow been saved and were available for purification, they could be used only sparingly. Levitical impurity thus became so widespread that the priests had to reconsider the status of the Heave-offering of wine and other fruit juices, as well as of olives.

Eliezer solved the whole problem with a sweeping declaration that "liquids are not susceptible to any form of impurity." The urgency which led to this decision is obvious from the fact that it runs counter to a specific statement in Scripture (Lev. 11:34) and certainly was opposed to the tradition of the day. It is especially noteworthy that Eliezer ben Hyrkanos, who boasted that he never gave an opinion which he had not received from his masters, should have been the author of this remarkable, and in a sense revolutionary, innovation. The proof he offered as basis for his interpretation of the Law effectually refutes him, as he himself must have recognized. He maintained that his rule was a corollary of a pronouncement made more than two hundred years earlier by Jose ben Joezer, one of the earliest Pharisaic teachers, who declared that the "liquids of the Temple slaughter-house are pure." Eliezer insisted that legally no distinction could be drawn between the liquids which Jose ben Joezer mentioned and others; if the old Pharisaic sages was correct so far as his rule went, then all liquids were pure.

It is obvious that an opponent of Eliezer might argue with equal, if not with greater cogency that Jose ben Joezer's words imply that other liquids are impure. But Eliezer, like the earlier Shammaites, did not listen to objections. Convinced, doubtless, that the ruling was indispensable and justified, he offered it to those who would follow him.

Aqiba, however, was unmoved by the plight of priest or provincial farmer. He knew that liquids had always been considered impure, and he could see no great reason for making a change in the tradition. On the contrary, he opposed even the attempt made by his colleagues to effect a compromise declaring liquids subject only to "rabbinical impurity."

Eliezer is described (p. 122) as a leading patrician figure: "His insolent bluntness, his stubborn insistence on his own infallibility, his total disregard of the rights of others, made him, in spite of his brilliant record, especially vulnerable." Therefore Joshua and Aqiba were able to have him excommunicated on the issue of "The Stove of the Serpent Rings," treated by Finkelstein as follows:

> Biblical law demands that earthenware pots and ovens which have become defiled, as for instance, by contact with a dead insect, be broken (Lev. 11:33). To circumvent this law, the prosperous had invented a "serpent stove," i.e., an oven which -- made of tiles, joined together by loose layers of earth -- could be taken apart and put together again. This procedure they called "breaking the oven." Eliezer, speaking for the wealthy farmers, who could afford such complicated utensils, defended the legal fiction. But the poorer scholars, who had to be satisfied with ordinary ovens, resented the subterfuge. They said that the oven would remain defiled unless it was actually broken. This view was defended by Joshua and adopted by the conclave. Eliezer continued to declare these ovens pure. When the conclave assembled to hear charges against Eliezer, Gamaliel found himself in a dilemma. He could not defend in his brother-in-law the defiance he had repressed in others. Moreover, Eliezer made no attempt to deny or mitigate the accusation; he merely insisted that he was right and all the others were wrong. Whatever may have been the original intention of Eliezer's accusers, his attitude drove them into a frenzy of anger, and they not only ousted him from the Sanhedrin, but expelled him from the Pharisaic order. Not for half a century had this punishment been meted out to a scholar.

The sociological and economic interpretations of Eliezer seem the most curious element in the legacy of earlier scholarship. They are frequently plausible, but never conclusive and compelling, and the mode of argument, in both Bokser's and Finkelstein's cases, consists of colorful narrative, accompanied by frequent reiteration of what is to begin with alleged, instead of an effort to show that what is alleged is not only plausible but also the best of many possible interpretations.

The whole approach therefore is to be regarded as a deductive mode of argument, in which an antecedent "principle" is illustrated through many cases, but independently demonstrated in none of them. As to the principal allegation, we have no decisive evidence that Eliezer was rich or that he was poor. His sayings, seen without preconceptions about his economic interests, seem to me to show neither that he was an aristocrat or patrician nor that he was a plebian or a commoner. That Lydda was "particularly popular with emigré aristocracy" was because Eliezer lived there. He lived there because he was an emigré aristocrat. Eliezer's role as a Shammaite is taken for granted, also his conservatism in law -- which proves his conservatism in everything else. Orthodox writer's piety about Eliezer's saintliness finds its counterpart in Bokser's and Finkelstein's impiety about his boorishness. The dramatic language employed in this connection -- "bullying at the slightest provocation" -- seems particularly odd.

The issues of Eliezer's opposition to individualism and universalism in theology are totally extraneous to the materials before us and seem, moreover, to be irrelevant even to the poorest traditions. Indeed, if we had not known that Eliezer was supposed to be opposed to individualism and universalism, we might not have grasped that these issues were implicit in his sayings, though admittedly, they possibly occur in a few of them. Eliezer's espousal of uniformity and stability seems exactly contrary to the tendencies we discern. As to his "mechanical application of the law," it is difficult to find evidence that he ever actually applied the law, mechanically or otherwise. The allegation as to Eliezer's class sympathies and the class struggle of his day is, to be sure, an important datum for the study of the history and sociology of Talmudic scholarship in the first half of the twentieth century.

Finkelstein likewise sees Eliezer as "ill-bred" and a provincial, "wont to utter...lurid curses..." This colorful language is enriched with such adjectives as "foppish." Finkelstein's plausible explanation of the problem of the ritual cleanness of olive oil and so on seems to go far beyond the limits of the evidence. Eliezer's opinion that liquids are not susceptible to uncleanness is interpreted by itself, without the detailed consideration of all other pericopae in which the problem arises. Instead, we are told that like the earlier Shammaites, Eliezer did not "listen to objections." The treatment of the problem would be more helpful if, instead of personal criticism of Eliezer, Finkelstein had raised the problems and "objections" to be considered in Eliezer's own pericopae. The interpretation of the Akhnai-oven is equally plausible, but also without the support of more evidence than the allegation that such might have been the case.

iv

A Biography of Eliezer?

All accounts[2] maintain the pretense that everything Eliezer is supposed to have said was actually stated by him, and everything he is alleged to have done actually happened. Since we have no grounds whatever for accepting these suppositions, we have to reject out of hand virtually every biographical statement in antecedent accounts, though interpretations of specific pericopae are not thereby rendered wholly valueless. But, overall, we cannot recover much of the biography of Eliezer b. Hyrcanus, even though materials purporting to relate his life-story are in our hands.

We have a substantial corpus of legal materials produced in the circles of Eliezer's disciples and associates, the existence of which seems adequately attested within decades of his death. These materials do not pertain to Eliezer's biography. To be sure, one may derive from them details, not all of them inconsequential, about where Eliezer lived, his station in life, his associates and his disciples. But were we to concentrate upon biographical details, we should neglect the primary and important historical facts before us, which consist of a small but a genuine account of some of Eliezer's opinions and rulings. Our study of the traditions cannot, therefore, be ignored in the formulation of a life of Eliezer. It must, on the contrary, impose the main outline of our inquiry. To the traditions about Eliezer we may then add other fairly dependable, independent evidence about the times in which he lived. Together these materials cannot produce a comprehensive history of the Yavnean period. But they do allow the formulation of a number of reasonably reliable statements about Eliezer as a historical figure.

So let us proceed to divide up the materials at hand by a simple criterion: which appear in earlier texts, those closer to his life, and which in later ones? What undergo discussion in texts that come near to his life and to the lifetime of his immediate disciples, and which do not? These we may then postulate give us better materials than others. Indeed, we may distinguish three Eliezers: the Eliezer of history, the Eliezer of tradition, and the Eliezer of legend. I offer the hypothesis only as a modest example of what sort of analytical work remains suggestive.

The Eliezer of history -- according to the hypothesis at hand -- is revealed by the best-attested, the better-attested , and some only fairly-well traditions. Best-attested materials occur in documents closed earliest, in particular, the Mishnah and in parts of the Tosefta contemporary with the formation of the Mishnah. These are to be divided into two parts. The best pericopae tell us what in the opinion of his successors Eliezer thought about a number of discrete legal issues. The better and the fair ones -- those in documents closed beyond the Mishnah's redaction, for example -- provide a picture of the legal issues he faced,

---

[2]In *Eliezer* I cite them at length.

but not necessarily of his actual opinions about them. One must therefore distinguish between the best and better materials, which reveal whatever we are likely to know about the Eliezer of history, and the fair ones, which constitute an extension of the former and give a picture of the Eliezer of living traditions. That is, the fair traditions portray the Eliezer seen by people in close touch with the evolving traditions begun in Eliezer's own circle of disciples and associates and their continuators.

We have in addition what I call poor traditions. They are the ones that surfacer only in documents redacted very late in the formation of the canon as a whole, and, further, that bear no clear relationship to any allegations concerning Eliezer in documents redacted early on. The poor traditions of various sorts portray the Eliezer of legend. They do not relate materials evolving out of Eliezer's life and circles of disciples and associates and their successors and continuators, but tell us only what much later masters thought important to say about Eliezer. As noted, in some circumstances one may argue that these materials are appropriate to the times of Eliezer and congruent to the range of problems he ought to have confronted.[3] They report things he might have said and should have done. They not merely fill in gaps in his portrait; they supply a full-length picture, giving a private life and a biography to a man hitherto known through policies and programs, but not revealed as a personality in his own right. To this affirmative -- if weak -- argument in behalf of their authenticity we may add a negative, slightly better one. The poor traditions tend not to attribute to Eliezer things which he "ought" not to have said; they do not tell us that he taught ideas important only later on. They exhibit little trace of the rabbinism developing in other circles in his own time and flourishing in all circles later on. The absence of "rabbinical" sayings, is striking evidence that the later tradents did not normally hand on in Eliezer's name materials they certainly could not have received from his living traditions. That does not mean what they did hand on certainly were things he actually said and stories redacted in his own day and under the hand of his disciples (or enemies). But it strongly suggests that the tradents normally did not deliberately anachronize in telling about Eliezer and in attributing sayings to him.

Let us close with a brief look backward at the historical representation of other figures of the first century. Until Eliezer, rabbinic heroes are known through traditions and legends, but not through historically reliable materials of any kind. That is to say, the criteria for admitting a statement about Eliezer to the arena of possibility exclude pretty much everything told about figures who lived prior to his time. For instance, of the historical Hillel nothing may be said. But the Hillel of later rabbinic legend is a fully developed figure. The other pre-70 Pharisaic masters are primarily figures of legend. The Houses of Shammai and Hillel produce legal traditions, many of them quite reliable, but

---

[3]Compare pp. 110-117.

the Houses do not constitute historical actors at all. They testify to the state of
Pharisaic law but report little about the activities of the Pharisaic group.

Yohanan b. Zakkai is the subject of legends but in addition stands behind
traditions of considerable interest.[4] If we take for granted that Yohanan was the
major figure in the establishment of the Yavnean institution after 70, then we
must be astonished at how little we have about him from Yohanan's own
associates and successors. The first important attestations of Yohanan's
materials come from authorities on the other side of Bar Kokhba's War, after
140, chiefly from Judah b. Ilai (but show no relationship to Eliezer). It is only
with the few appearances of Yohanan in Mishnah-Tosefta that we see the
beginning of a significant corpus of materials about him. Then, in the legendary
stage, Yohanan is given a full repertoire of sayings and stories. He gets the
major role in the siege of Jerusalem and the later negotiations with the Romans.
He is made into a dominant historical figure. The silence of the Yavneans and
most later figures for a hundred or more years should tell us the historical
Yohanan b. Zakkai was an unimportant figure at best. But the facts of history
require a quite contrary view, even though the legends which purport to describe
the course of events have little to recommend them, beyond their prima facie
plausibility. While, therefore, with reference to Yohanan b. Zakkai, we could
speak of a figure as revealed chiefly by traditions (of varying worth) and a
character portrayed primarily by legend (mostly late and imaginary), in Eliezer
we perceive in addition a historical actor, and one of the first importance. But to
end where we began, precisely what history we are to learn from the stories and
sayings about Eliezer remains subject to debate. I contend that with some effort
we may identify a few substantial facts. Others maintain that it is all true. And
that, to end this prologue to our own time, is what the fight is all about.

---

[4]I refer to my *Development of a Legend. Studies on the Traditions Concerning Yohanan ben
Zakkai* (Leiden, 1970: E. J. Brill).

Part Three

THE OLD GULLIBILITY *REDIVIVUS*

Chapter Four

Reading, Believing, and Historical Study.
Some Choice Examples in Current Scholarship

i

Definition of Historical Gullibility in the Study of the History of Ancient Jews and Judaism

I argue not with what people think but how they frame their questions and reach their conclusions. No one can argue with a position that to begin with rests on false premises as to the character of the sources. If questions rest on the premise that sources at hand contain answers to those questions, then the framing of the questions rests on a premise as to the character of the evidence at hand. I propose to specify that premise, working backward from the questions or conclusions before us to the information the scholars at hand assume the sources provide. My examples therefore serve to demonstrate not wrong opinions but incorrect methods, which make results irrelevant.

In historical debate, we gain access to no knowledge *a priori*. All facts derive from sources correctly situated, e.g., classified, comprehensively and completely described, dispassionately analyzed, and evaluated. Nothing can be taken for granted. What we cannot show, we do not know. These simple dogmas of all historical learning derive not from this writer but go back to the very beginnings of Western critical historical scholarship, to the age of the Renaissance. When the Donation of Constantine proved false, all received facts of a historical character stood at risk. These same principles -- *"it ain't necessarily so, /it ain't necessarily so, /the things that you're liable /to read in the Bible -- /it ain't necessarily so"* -- emerged with new sharpness from the mind of Spinoza, who founded modern critical biblical scholarship. They passed through the purifying skepticism of the Enlightenment, which learned -- because it had to -- how to laugh. But gullibility suffered a still further blow in the nineteenth century's refounding of historical science. Systematic skepticism illuminated the founders of historical sciences in the nineteenth century. They serve as commonplace models in the twentieth. Anyone who claims to tell us what happened a long time ago obeys these simple rules, and no one who ignores them can properly use the past tense. At issue is not personal conviction -- fundamentalism in a theological sense, of which I accuse no one in this book -- but public principles of inquiry. At issue are matters of public inquiry, not available for idiosyncratic and private apologia through a mere: "I believe." When the fundamentalist states, "I believe," he makes a statement of profound consequence. When a gullible scholar claims that the "burden of proof is on the doubter," he violates the language-rules of his professed field and says something that is merely silly.

Source analysis (beginning with the classification and characterization of documents, as, in Chapter Five, I propose to be the central task) is the beginning of all historical work. It tells us what we know, what we might know, and what we do not know, about the period of which the source claims to present information. No serious historical narrative, let alone analysis, can undertake a proposition without analysis of sources: telling what they are, what they convey, and why they are to be believed *or disbelieved*. Nor do we know how to engage in debate with one who, without systematic critical description of the whole, reads sources as though they record things really said or done by those to whom sayings are imputed and deeds attributed. And, it goes without saying, scholars who purport to tell us not what the source says but what really was, or must have been, going on in the mind of the historical actor in the fairy-tale, if they claim to tell us history, misunderstand the profession ("He must have said...," "he undoubtedly did not ..."). For they were not there. Scholars who begin with a hypothesis, by mid-paragraph have turned the hypothesis into a fact, and at the end of the paragraph announce that they have now proved the facticity of their original hypothesis do not present well-crafted arguments of a critical character.

In other fields of historical and historical-religious study, until we know what sort of information a source tells us, we cannot find the appropriate location of that source at a particular place and time. We do not establish the context in which information has been recorded solely by reading the words before us. And if we do not know the situation about which the source actually testifies, we also cannot correctly grasp the context of the historical information that the source indubitably conveys to us. Hence we cannot evaluate or accurately describe the fact that the text purports to convey: something about its own time, something about past time. So if someone claims to know what was said and done in the second century but proves it from sources of the sixth (as does nearly every writer we shall read), we cannot evaluate that person's claim -- the proposition at hand -- without first understanding how that person has analyzed the evidence. These constitute the givens of all scholarly research. Any other premises lay the foundations for impressionistic and theological disquisition, not historical description, analysis, and interpretation. For the contrary premise is that there are things we can know without showing how we know them, that is, *a priori* knowledge. In religion, yes, but in historical study, no.

Let me rapidly restate what I mean by gullibility in the academic context. Two traits of mind define academic gullibility.

One is believing everything you read.

The second is free-associating about what you read, without the control of a test of right or wrong.

If I believe without asking how does the author of this text knows that the things he imputes to an authority really were said by that authority, hence at the time that that authority lived, I am as gullible as a fundamentalist. In the setting of the rabbinic writings of late antiquity, if I take for granted that what is attributed to a given rabbi really was said by him, in his day, when he lived, and recorded verbatim from that day until it was written down, and if -- and this proves the premise on which I work -- on that basis I say what happened in that rabbi's time, then I am credulous. And if not, then I am not.

ii

**Examples of Historical Gullibility
in New Testament Scholarship:
Helmut Koester on the Historical Hillel and
E. P. Sanders on "the Rabbis"**

Helmut Koester, *Introduction to the New Testament*. I. *History, Culture, and Religion of the Hellenistic Age* (Philadelphia, 1982: Fortress Press, and Berlin and New York, 1982,. Walter DeGruyter. Translated from the German *Einfuehrung in das Neue Testament,* Berlin, 1980: Walter de Gruyter) I, p. 406, states:

> **Hillel.** What would give to later rabbinic Judaism its characteristic mark was the practice of legal interpretation in the Babylonian synagogue. Hillel (who lived until about 20 CE) came from Babylon. He may have also studied in Jerusalem, but his exegetical principles, which together with his humaneness became determinative for rabbinic Judaism, reveal the diaspora situation, for which legislation related to the temple cult and to living conditions in an overwhelmingly Jewish country were of only academic interest. This perspective as well as his great gifts as a teacher made Hillel the father of rabbinic Judaism -- much more so than his famous exegetical rules, like the conclusion a minore ad maius and the conclusion from analogy. In contrast, his often-quoted opponent Shammai represents a branch of Pharisaism which was closely related to the temple. Shammai is aristocratic, severe, and nationalistic. But Gamaliel I, Hillel's successor as the head of his school (probably a son of Hillel) had also become a member of the Jerusalem aristocracy. He was a member of the Jerusalem sanhedrin who became famous for his wisdom (and as such he appears in Acts 5:34-39), though he may have distanced himself sometimes from the prevailing opinion of that institution, as is indicated by the report of the Book of Acts. However, Gamaliel's son Simeon became the leader of the Pharisaic war party and was associated with the first government of the revolutionaries, although he later had to make room for a more radical leadership. This Pharisaic war party can be largely identified with the Shammaites with whom Simeon, grandson of Hillel, perished in the chaos of the Jewish war.

Koester presents a pastiche of allusions to references to Hillel in a diverse body of writings, some of them separated from the time in which Hillel lived by only two hundred years, others by much longer. For example, "Hillel the Babylonian" and merely "Hillel" do not occur side by side. Should we not ask whether, overall, "Hillel-the-Babylonian" references present a viewpoint about Hillel different from the "merely-Hillel" sources? "His" exegetical principles are assigned to him only in sources of the fourth century and beyond -- four hundred years later. Does Koester describe the life of Jesus on the basis of statements of fourth century Church fathers? I think not. The conclusion *a minore ad maius*, for example, is a commonplace in Scripture and not Hillel's invention. I can direct him to chapter and verse, both in Scripture and in the later rabbinic exegesis of Scripture. For more than a few passages in the canon of Judaism recognize that fact. Koester even favors us with the gentle and humane Hillel, in the tradition of the stories, obviously partisan, that contrast the humane Hillel and the captious Shammai -- stories that, in the main, circulated only in the latest parts of the canon. Then, with "But Gamaliel...," we jump into a different body of sources, now drawing on Josephus and Acts for the rest of the tale. So we mix up a rather diverse group of sources,some from the first century, some from the seventh, believing whatever we find in any one of them, and forming the whole into a harmonious statement.

In his *Paul and Palestinian Judaism: A Comparison of Patterns of Religion* (London, 1977: SCM Press), E. P. Sanders cites as evidence for opinions held in the first century documents redacted long afterward. The reason is that those documents contain sayings attributed to first century figures. Even by 1973 (the year in which his work was completed) it was clear that the issue of historical dependability of attributions of sayings to particular rabbis had to be faced, even though, admittedly, it had not been faced in most of the work on which Sanders was able to draw. The issues of historical evidence should enter into the notion of the comparison of systems, such as Sanders claims to undertake. If it should turn out that "the Rabbis'" ideas about a given theological topic respond to a historical situation subject to fairly precise description, then the work of comparison becomes still more subtle and precarious. For if "the Rabbis" address their thought -- for example, about the right motive for the right deed -- to a world in which, in the aftermath of a terrible catastrophe, the issue of what it is that human beings still control is central, the comparison of their thought to that of Paul requires us to imagine what Paul *might have said* if confronted by the situation facing "the Rabbis." If we have a saying assigned to Aqiba how do we know it really was said by him, belonging to the late first and early second century? If we cannot show that it does go back to A.D. 100, then we are not justified in adducing such sayings as evidence of the state of mind of one late-first- and early-second-century authority, let alone of *all* the late-first- and early-second-century authorities -- and let alone of "the Rabbis" of the later first and whole of the second centuries. I cannot concede that Sanders' notion of systemic description, even if it were wholly effected, has removed from the critical agendum these simple questions of historical study we have yet to answer. This provides a fine example of what is at stake in gullibility.

Nor should we ignore the importance in the work of establishing the historical context in which the saying was said (or at least in which it was important to be quoted). Sanders many times cites the famous saying attributed to Yohanan b. Zakkai that the corpse does not contaminate, nor does purification water purify, but the whole thing is hocus-pocus. That saying first occurs in a later, probably fourth-century, Midrashic compilation. Surely we might wonder whether, at the time of the making of that compilation, issues of magic were not central in Rabbinic discourse. I assemble the evidence on rabbinical wonder-working (magic) in the period under discussion in my *History of the Jews in Babylonia*, vol. 3, *From Shapur I to Shapur II* (Leiden, 1968), pp. 102-30; vol. 4, *The Age of Shapur II* (Leiden, 1969), pp. 330-63; and vol. 5, *Later Sasanian Times* (Leiden, 1970), pp. 174-93. There is some indication that more wonder-working or magical stories are told about third- and fourth-century rabbis than about second-century ones, and this corresponds to a general rise in magical activity. The denial of efficacy, *ex opere operato*, of a scriptural purification rite, addressed to a world in which magic, including Torah magic, was deemed to work *ex opere operato*, may be interpreted as a powerful polemic against a strong current of the fourth-century Palestinian and Babylonian Jews' life, a time at which Rabbinical circles, among others, were deeply interested in the magical powers inherent in Torah. Now I do not mean to suggest that the proper interpretation of the saying is in accord with this hypothesis, nor do I even propose the stated hypothesis for serious consideration here. I only offer it as an example of one context in which the saying is credibly to be interpreted and, more important, as evidence of the centrality of context in the interpretation of each and every saying. If we do not know where and when a saying was said, how are we to interpret the saying and explain its meaning?

Had Sanders presented a nuanced picture of the diverse Judaisms of the age, including the diverse characteristics of the systems represented by rabbinic compilations and compositions (of which his knowledge is elementary), he could not have done the work he wished to do. Nonetheless, gullibility exacts its charge on Sanders' work. In my view the meaning of a saying is defined, at the outset, by the context in which it is meaningful. To be sure, the saying may remain meaningful later on, so that, cited for other purposes, the saying takes on new meanings. No one denies that obvious proposition, which, after all, is illustrated best of all by the history of the interpretation, but, of greater systemic consequence, the deliberate misinterpretation, of the Old Testament in Judaism and Christianity. If that is so, then we surely should not reduce to a single, limited hermeneutical framework the interpretation by sayings attributed to rabbis in Rabbinic documents of diverse periods, put together, as I said earlier, for diverse purposes and therefore addressed, it seems to me self-evident, to historically diverse circumstances.

Throughout his "constructive" discussions of Rabbinic ideas about theology, Sanders quotes all documents equally with no effort at differentiation among them. He seems to have culled sayings from the diverse sources he has chosen and written them down on cards, which he proceeded to organize around his critical categories. Then he has constructed his paragraphs and sections by flipping through those cards and commenting on this and that. So there is no context in which a given saying is important in its own setting, in its own document. No wonder in his sequel to his book he found himself unable to deal with the criticisms presented here.

Finally, we note that while even the most primitive New Testament scholars will concur that we must pay attention to the larger purposes of the several evangelists in citing sayings assigned to Jesus in the various Gospels, Sanders fails to differentiate among documents. They are all the same, and we may quote them without differentiation among them. Everyone knows that if we ignore Matthew's theory of the law and simply extract Matthew's versions of Jesus' sayings about the law and set them up side by side with the sayings about the law given to Jesus by other of the evangelists and attitudes imputed to him by Paul, we create a mess of contradictions. Why then should the context of diverse Rabbinic sayings, for example, on the law, be ignored?

iii

Example of Historical Gullibility in the Study of the History of the Jews: Shaye J. D. Cohen on Yavneh

Shaye J. D. Cohen, "The Significance of Yavneh: Pharisees, Rabbis, and the End of Jewish Sectarianism," *Hebrew Union College Annual* 55, 1984, pp. 27-53 presents an important thesis. In order to make certain he is represented accurately, I cite his own précis of his article, which is as follows:

> After the destruction of the second temple in 70 C.E. the rabbis gathered in Yavneh and launched the process which yielded the Mishnah approximately one hundred years later. Most modern scholars see these rabbis as Pharisees triumphant, who define "orthodoxy," expel Christians and other heretics, and purge the canon of "dangerous" books. The evidence for this reconstruction is inadequate. In all likelihood most of the rabbis were Pharisees, but there is no indication that the rabbis of the Yavnean period were motivated by a Pharisaic self-consciousness (contrast the Babylonian Talmud and the medieval polemics against the Karaites) or were dominated by an exclusivistic ethic. In contrast the major goal of the Yavnean rabbis seems to have been not the expulsion of those with whom they disagreed but the cessation of sectarianism and the creation of a society which tolerated, even encouraged, vigorous debate among members of the fold. The Mishnah is the first work of Jewish antiquity which ascribes conflicting legal opinions to named individuals who, in spite of their disagreements, belong to the same fraternity. This mutual tolerance is the enduring legacy of Yavneh.

Now what is important is not Cohen's theory, with which I do not undertake an argument, but whether or not to formulate and prove his theory, he consistently and rigorously asks the fundamental questions of criticism: how do I know whether it is so. Here he asks that question only inconsistently, as I shall show.

Let us now proceed to ask how Cohen uses the evidence, investigating the theory of the character of the sources that leads him to frame his questions in one way and not in some other. What we shall see, first of all, is that Cohen takes at face value the historical allegation of a source that a given rabbi made the statement attributed to him. At pp. 32-33 Cohen states:

> The text narrates a story about a Sadducee and a high priest, and concludes with the words of the wife of the Sadducee:
>
> A.   Although they [= we] are wives of Sadducees, they [= we] fear the Pharisees and show their [= our] menstrual blood to the sages."
>
> B.   R. Yosi says, "We are more expert in them [Sadducean women] than anyone else. They show (menstrual) blood to the sages, except for one woman who was in our neighborhood, who did not show her (menstrual blood to the sages, and she died [immediately]" (Bab. Niddah 33b).

Cohen forthwith states, "In this text there is chronological tension between parts A and B. A clearly refers to a woman who lived during second temple times, while B has R. Yose derive his expertise about Sadducean women from personal acquaintance." Why Cohen regards that "tension" as probative or even pertinent I cannot say. Now we may wonder whether Cohen believes Yose really made the statement attributed him. We note that Cohen does not specify the point at which "the text" was redacted. The fact that the Babylonian Talmud reached closure in the sixth or seventh century makes no difference. *If the text refers to Yose, then it testifies to the second century, not to the seventh.*

We shall now hear Cohen treat the text as an accurate report of views held in the time of which it speaks. How does he know? Because the text says so: it refers to this, it refers to that. What we have is a newspaper reporter, writing down things really said and giving them over to the National Archives for preservation until some later reporter chooses to add to the file: a clear instance of gullibility indeed. Here is Cohen again, in the same passage, starting with the pretense of a critical exercise of analysis:

> In this text there is chronological tension between parts A and B. A clearly refers to a woman who lived during second temple times, while B has R. Yosi derive his expertise about Sadducean women from personal acquaintance. He recalls a Sadducean woman who lived in his neighborhood and died prematurely because (R. Yosi said) she did not accept the authority of the sages to determine her menstrual status.

To this point Cohen simply paraphrases the text, and now he will verify the story. It seems to me that Cohen takes for granted Yose really made the saying attributed to him, and, moreover, that saying is not only Yose's view of matters, but how matters really were. He says so in so many words: "This baraita clearly implies that R. Yosi is referring to contemporary Saducean women. If this is correct, R. Yosi's statement shows that some Sadducees still existed in the mid-second century but that their power had declined to the extent that the rabbis could assume that most Sadducees follow rabbinic norms." It seems to me beyond doubt that Cohen takes for granted that what is attributed to Yose really was said by him, and, more interestingly, Yose testifies to how things were not in one place but everywhere in the country. "If this is correct" Cohen concludes not that Yose *thought* there were still a few Sadducees around, but that there *were* still a few Sadducees around. There is a difference. Cohen does not tell us what conclusions he draws *if this is not correct,* because, in point of fact, that possibility he declines to explore.

Nonetheless, he wants to verify the story. How? By finding another text that tells the same story:

> The version of the Tosefta is similar:
> A.   "Although we are Sadducean women, we all consult a sage."
> B.   R. Yosi says, "We are more expert in Saducean women that anyone else: they all consult a sage except for one who was among them, and she died" (Tosefta Niddah 5:3).
>
> The Tosefta does not identify Pharisees with sages, a point to which we shall return below, and omits the phrase "who was in our neighborhood." Otherwise, it is basically, the same as the Babylonian version.

Now the reader may rightly wonder, perhaps Cohen intends something other than historical narrative about views Yose held or opinions he taught. Maybe Cohen proposes to write a history of the tradition about a given matter. In that case simply citing this and that serves a valid purpose. I concur.

But Cohen leaves no doubt as to his intention. Let us listen as he tells us what *really* happened: since Yose made his statement, Yose's statement tells us about the second century. Then Yose's statement proves that there were Sadducees in the mid-second century but they had no power. I find no evidence whatsoever that Cohen grasps the critical problem of evaluating the allegations of sources. He looks into a source and comes up with a fact. If he finds two versions of the same story, the fact is still more factual. And, if that were not enough, he gives us the "proof" of "according to rabbinic tradition." That tradition suffices: "They always failed, of course, but they resisted; by the second century they stopped resisting." Let us review those clear statements of his:

> This baraita clearly implies that R. Yosi is referring to contemporary Sadducean women. If this is correct, R. Yosi's statement shows that some Sadducees still existed in the mid-second century but that their power had declined to the extent that the rabbis could assume that most Sadducees follow rabbinic norms. Contrast the Sadducees of the second temple period who, according to rabbinic tradition, tried to resist rabbinic hegemony (see below). They always failed, of course, but they resisted: by the second century they stopped resisting. This is the perspective of R. Yosi.

The "if this is correct" changes nothing. As soon as the "if" has been said, it is treated as a "then." "Then" it is correct, so Cohen here tells us the story of the Sadducees in the first and second centuries. In the first century they resisted "rabbinic norms," whatever they were, but in the second century, they gave up. This is Cohen's conclusion, based on his failure to ask how the Bavli and the Tosefta's compilers or the author of the story at hand knew the facts of the matter. The sole undisputed fact is that they represent the facts one way, rather than some other. But that does not suffice.

Let us see how he analyzes sources. At p. 42 he says:

> Rabbinic tradition is aware of opposition faced by Yohanan ben Zakkai at Yavneh but knows nothing of any expulsion of these opponents (Bab. Rosh Hashanah 2b). Yohanan ben Zakkai was even careful to avoid a confrontation with the priests (Mishnah 'Eduyyot 8:3).

Now what have we here? "Rabbinic tradition" indeed. What can that possibly mean? All rabbis at all times? A particular rabbi at a given time? Church historians these days rarely base their historical facts on "the tradition of the Church." Would that we could write a life of Jesus based on the tradition of the Church, how many problems we could solve. Cohen does not favor us with an exercise in differentiation among the sources. His is an undifferentiated harmony of the Jewish Gospels. Indeed, to the opposite, he looks into "rabbinic tradition," undifferentiated, unanalyzed, and gives us a fact: *Bab. Rosh Hashanah 2b*. What can that be? It is a story about someone. What does the story tell us? Is it true? Why should we think so? Cohen does not ask these questions. He alludes to a page in the Talmud, and that constitutes his fact, on which, it goes without saying, he proposes to build quite an edifice. So the Talmud is a kind of telephone book, giving us numbers through which we make our connections. In no way does he establish a critical method which tells us why he believes what he believes and disbelieves what he rejects.

But he does have a clear theory of matters. Where sources concur with Cohen's thesis, he accepts them, and where not, not. Cohen wants to prove that earlier there were disputes, later on disputes ended. Now some sources say that earlier there were no disputes, later on there were disputes. *So Cohen rejects the historicity of the sources that say there were no disputes earlier and accepts that of the ones that say there were no disputes later.*   This sleight of hand I find on p. 48. Here he cites T. Hagigah 2:9, "At first there was no dispute in Israel." He proceeds to point to an "irenic trend," Mishnah Yevamot 1:4 and Eduyyot 4:8, which alleges that while the Houses disputed various matters, they still intermarried and respected each other's conformity to the purity rules. Then Cohen: "But this wishful thinking cannot disguise the truth. The two Talmudim find it almost impossible to understand this statement. The Houses could not marry or sup with each other. They were virtually sects -- kitot the Palestinian Talmud calls them (Yer. Hagigah 2:2). At Yavneh sectarian exclusiveness was replaced by rabbinic pluralism, collective authority was replaced by individual authority."

What Cohen has done is to reject the statements in *earlier* sources -- Mishnah, Tosefta -- and adopt those in *later* ones (the Palestinian Talmud). He has done so simply by fiat. He cites what they say, and then he calls it wishful thinking. The truth, he discovers, is in the judgment of the Palestinian Talmud. I find this strange, for two reasons.

First, it is odd to reject the testimony of the earlier source, closer to the situation under discussion, in favor of the later.

Second, it is not entirely clear why and how Cohen knows that the Mishnah's and Tosefta's statements represent wishful thinking at all.

Had he cited the talmudic discussions of the passage, readers would have found that the problem confronting the later exegetes is not quite what Cohen says it was. The Talmuds do not say that the parties were "virtually sects." That statement, it is true, occurs where Cohen says it does -- but that is not on the passage of M. Yevamot 1:4 etc. that Cohen is discussing. It is on another passage entirely. The talmudic discussion on the Mishnah-passage and its Tosefta-parallel is a legal one; the sages are troubled by the statement that people who disagree on laws of marriage and of purity can ignore those laws. The Talmudic discussion in no way sustains Cohen's statement. If now we reread the sequence of sentences, we find an interesting juxtaposition:

1.   The two Talmudim find it almost impossible to understand this statement.
2.   The Houses could not marry or sup with each other. They were virtually sects -- kitot the Palestinian Talmud calls them.
3.   At Yavneh sectarian exclusiveness was replaced by rabbinic pluralism, collective authority was replaced by individual authority.

Now sentence three does not follow from sentence two, unless sentence two has had something to do with "sectarian exclusiveness" replaced by "rabbinic pluralism." But the passage cited by Cohen does not say that, it has no bearing on that proposition. Cohen writes as though the evidence supports his thesis, when, in fact, the evidence has no bearing on that thesis. The sentences in fact do not follow from one another. No. 1 is factually inaccurate. No. 2 makes the valid point that the Yerushalmi calls the sects *kitot*. That is an undisputed fact. It however bears no consequences for the statements fore or aft. And no. 3 is parachuted down, Cohen's own judgment. So, to repeat, he accepts as a matter of fact the *later* sources' allegations, rejects the *earlier* sources' statements, finds in a source not related to anything a statement he wishes to believe, cites that, then repeats -- as though it had been proved -- the fundamental thesis of his paper.

It follows that Cohen's reading of the source begins with a generous view of the *a priori* accuracy of his own convictions about what the source is saying. Yohanan's "care" in avoiding a confrontation is Cohen's allegation, for the source does not quite say that. It says, in point of fact, not that he avoided confrontation, but that he did not think he could force the priests to do what they refused to do. That is the exact language of the source. Now the statement imputed to Yohanan ben Zakkai may mean he was careful about avoiding confrontation. It may also mean he did not feel like wasting his time on lost causes. It may mean a great many other things. Cohen simply cites the tractate and its chapter and paragraph number, and lo, another fact, another proof. Once more, a properly incredulous reader must wonder whether I misrepresent the facts about Cohen's gullibility.

I shall now show that Cohen can tell us "the truth," because *he* knows which source is giving us facts and which source is giving us fancies. That explains why what gets a question -mark "(at Yavneh?)" half a dozen lines later loses the question-mark and becomes a fact: "At Yavneh sectarian exclusiveness was replaced by rabbinic pluralism." On what basis? Let us hear. For this purpose we review the materials just now set forth. At pp. 48-49 he says:

Some of the rabbis were aware that their ideology of pluralism did not exist before 70. "At first there was no dispute (mahloqet) in Israel" (Tos. Hagigah 2:9 and Sanhedrin 7:1). How did disputes begin? According to one view in the Tosefta, disputes were avoided by the adjudication of the great court which sat in the temple precincts and determined either by vote or by tradition the status of all doubtful matters. In this view, when the great court was destroyed in 70, disputes could no longer be resolved in an orderly way and mahloqot proliferated. According to another view, "once the disciples of Hillel and Shammai became numerous who did not serve [their masters] adequately, they multiplied disputes in Israel and became as two Torahs." In this view Jewish (i.e., rabbinic) unanimity was upset by the malfeasance of the disciples of Hillel and Shammai, a confession which would later be exploited by the Karaites. What happened to the disputes between the Houses? They ceased at Yavneh, how we do not know. Amoraic tradition (Yer. Yevamot 1:6 [3b] and parallels) tells of a heavenly voice which declared at Yavneh, "Both these [House of Hillel] and these [House of Shammai] are the words of the living God, but the halakha always follows the House of Hillel." As part of this irenic trend someone (at Yavneh?) even asserted that the disputes between the Houses did not prevent them from intermarrying or from respecting each other's purities (Mishnah Yevamot 1:4 and 'Eduyyot 4:8; Tos. Yevamot 1:10-12) but this wishful thinking cannot disguise the truth. The two Talmudim find it almost impossible to understand this statement. The Houses could not marry or sup with each other. They were virtually sects -- *kitot* the Palestinian Talmud calls them (Yer. Hagigah 2:2 [77d]). At Yavneh sectarian exclusiveness was replaced by rabbinic pluralism, collective authority was replaced by individual authority. The new ideal was the sage who was ready not to insist upon the rectitude of ("stand upon") his opinions. The creation of the Mishnah could now begin.

This repeated reading of Cohen's statements allows me to avoid the charge of quoting him out of context or only in part. I believe I have quoted him accurately, verbatim, and in context. So let us review the substance of the case.

When Cohen says, "...were aware," he treats the thesis of his article as the fact of the matter. Who were these rabbis? And how do we know of what they were, or were not, aware? Did they live at Yavneh, in 70? Or did they live in the early third century, when the Mishnah had reached closure, or did they live a hundred years later, when the Tosefta was coming to conclusion? Cohen does not tell us. But he clearly thinks that their awareness is evidence of historical fact. Now these in the aggregate constitute historical statements, e.g., "the Houses were virtually sects." Why Cohen valorizes Y. Hag. 2:2 -- a late source -- and dismisses the evidence of the Mishnah and Tosefta is something that causes a measure of surprise. In fact he has set out to prove at the end of his paragraph the very point he takes for granted at the outset of his paragraph. Philosophers call that begging the question.

Cohen's review of the stories makes a feint toward criticism. He cites diverse views, balancing one view against another. But from Cohen we do not have a history of peoples' opinions, we have facts. "What happened to the disputes between the Houses? They ceased at Yavneh, how we do not know." Here Cohen tells us that Neusner has shown that some of "the House disputes were later scholarly constructs, but these are not our concern." I do not know why it is not our concern. The Mishnah contains substantial evidence that the names of the Houses served to identify positions held by later disputants, of the mid-second century it would appear. Materials deriving from the period after the Bar Kokhba War are particularly rich in allusions to Houses' disputes that take up moot principles otherwise debated entirely in the age beyond Bar Kokhba's war. We clearly have mid-second century literary conventions. I do not mean to suggest that the names of the Houses served as more than literary conventions; I demonstrated that they served at least as literary conventions. Why? Were there "Houses of Shammai and Houses of Hillel" in the time of Yose, in the mid-second century? Is that why so many sayings about the relationships among the Houses are assigned, in fact, to mid-second century authorities? But the assignments of those sayings occur in documents edited only in the third century, at which point (some stories have it) the patriarch, Judah, discovered that he descended from Hillel. So perhaps the disputes of the Houses served a polemical purpose of the patriarchate, since the ancestor of the patriarchate -- everyone knew -- kept winning the disputes. These are only possibilities. In answering the question as Cohen phrases it, all we have are possibilities, few of them subject to tests of falsification or validation.

Cohen knows facts, the unbelieving among the rest of us, only possibilities. But why in particular much more than half a century beyond the point at which Cohen knows the Houses went out of business: "They ceased at Yavneh, how we do not know." Well, just what ceased at Yavneh, if the names of the Houses persisted as literary conventions and points of polemic for a hundred years and more.

Let us review in sequence Cohen's statements:

1.   But this wishful thinking cannot disguise the truth
2.   At Yavneh sectarian exclusiveness was replaced by rabbinic pluralism, collective authority was replaced by individual authority
3.   The new ideal was the sage who was ready not to insist upon the rectitude of his opinions.
4.   The creation of the Mishnah could now begin.

All of these statements may well be true. But in the paragraph I have cited, in which these statements occur, not a single source, not a single piece of evidence, proves any such thing. I cite No. 1 to prove that Cohen claims to make a historical statement. No. 2 then tells us he sees a movement from sect to church (though he does not appear to have read Max Weber, who saw much the same movement). Cohen has not proved that the "new ideal" of the sage antedates the Mishnah, in which it is said that that is the ideal. But he has ignored the fact that the Mishnah imputes that irenic position to none other than the House of Hillel -- who lived long before "Yavneh." And what all this has to do with "the creation of the Mishnah" only Cohen knows. So, in a climax of total confusion, if a passage in the *Mishnah* refers to the time of the Houses, but Cohen thinks that the fact does *not* apply to the time of the Houses, he ignores the allegation of the Mishnah's passage. If a passage in the Yerushalmi, two hundred years later, refers to the earlier period and says what Cohen thinks was the fact, then that later passage is true while the earlier one is not.

What does he do in the case at hand? He assigns that allegation neither to the context of the age of the Mishnah itself, as, to begin with, I would find plausible, nor to the age of which the passage itself speaks, namely, the time of the Houses (before 70, so Cohen), as other believers, consistent in their gullibility, would insist. In Cohen's mind, the passage testifies to an age of which it does not speak, and also in which the document that contains the passage was not redacted. We already have noticed that if a passage in a later rabbinic document refers to an earlier time and Cohen does think the fact applies to that early time, then he of course produces the source to prove the point that, to begin with, he wishes to make. So he prefers the later source that conforms to his thesis over the earlier one that does not.

Example of Historical Gullibility
in the Study of the History of Judaism:
Lawrence H. Schiffman on Who Was a Jew

We turn aside and review how the Talmud evaluates the historical context in which a saying was recorded. Here we first encounter what I call "the argument from contents." We shall see it many times again. My case for Schiffman's approach to rabbinic texts as gullibility rests on the claim that it recapitulates a mode of argument current in the Talmud of Babylonia in the sixth or seventh. So we turn first to the Talmud, and come back, in due course, to Schiffman's work.

When confronted with several versions of the same story, the authorities of the Babylonian Talmud whom we shall shortly read pretend to account for the inclusion of each detail of a saying or story -- among a variety of diverse details -- by making up a theory on where and how, by whom and for what purpose, a given detail "might" or "would" have been added. Let me spell out this approach because it is characteristic of the last century of scholarship and stands as the foundation of much work even now. So the entire analysis rests on the allegations of the text, construed, to begin with, as facts. Then we make up situations that account for these facts, and lo -- history. That is what I mean by an argument from contents.

When we have a long sequence of versions of a single matter, for instance the vision of the chariot described by Ezekiel as that vision was interpreted by Eleazar b. Azariah to Yohanan b. Zakkai, each successive shift and change in the version appearing in the earliest document to contain it will demand, and receive, a manufactured explanation. The assumption that each detail testifies to a given historical event or moment, different from other details in the same literary construct, rests on two premises.

First, the details -- it is postulated -- represent things that really happened, e.g., were really said by the person to whom they are attributed. So the premise reveals that same literalist gullibility that allegedly modern historians reject.

Second, it is assumed that the text at hand from the beginning was preserved exactly as it was written. Any change exhibited by a later version of a saying or story has, therefore, to find its explanation in a later event or a fresh setting. Changes do not just happen, they are made, and therefore for reason. The people who make them do so for reasons that the scholar can report (as we shall see, commonly on the basis of no evidence whatsoever).

Nothing lacks "significance" of a historical sort, and everything demands its explanation. No explanation covers everything; each item demands an *ad hoc* interpretation of its own. So the text is studded with histories, each supplied for its distinct occasion, none proposing to harmonize with or relate to the last or the next. Accordingly, it is theorized, people took a text and rewrote it as new things happened or in new circumstances. They then handed it on to others who did the same.

This literary theory awaits any sort of sustained argumentation, not to mention documentation. But it generates such scholarship as now flourishes on the problem at hand. What I think becomes clear is that this theory, which I call that of "incremental history," is "talmudic" in the worst sense. That is, it is *ad hoc*, merely made up, just as the Talmud itself makes up history, to explain several versions of one saying. Indeed, for all its claim to think in fresh and free ways, the newest generation, as represented here, botches the work.

Sages of ancient times recognized that sayings and stories appeared in diverse versions. They proposed explanations of how a given saying or story could come down in more than a single statement. The principal approach to the question posited that each detail represented a different stage in the history of the story, or of the life of its hero in particular, with one version characteristic of one such stage, and another version attesting to a different, and later one. So the successive versions of a saying or story supply a kind of incremental history. How so? Each version tells something about concrete events and real lives (biographies) that earlier versions did not reveal.

The classic Talmudic expression of the incremental theory takes up a passage of the Mishnah in which Rabban Yohanan ben Zakkai is called merely "Ben Zakkai:"

Mishnah Sanhedrin 5:2B

The precedent is as follows: Ben Zakkai examined a witness as to the character of the stalks of figs [under which an incident now subject to court procedure was alleged to have taken place].

As we shall now see, at paragraph N in the following talmudic analysis, exactly the same story is reported, on Tannaite authority. Now Rabban Yohanan ben Zakkai is alleged to have made exactly the same ruling, in exactly the same case. The item is worded in the same way except for the more fitting title. Then, at P-Q, the two versions are readily explained as facts of history. The one of Ben Zakkai was framed when he was a mere disciple. When, later on, he had become a recognized sage, the story was told to take account of that fact. So the theory I call "incremental history" is simple: each story related to, because it derives from, historical moments in a linear progression. The Talmudic passage is as follows:

IX. A. Who is this "Ben Zakkai"?
   B. If we should proposed that it is R. Yohanan ben Zakkai, did he ever sit in a sanhedrin [that tried a murder case]?
   C. And has it not been taught on Tannaite authority:

D. The lifetime of R. Yohanan ben Zakkai was a hundred and twenty years. For forty years he engaged in trade, for forty years he studied [Torah], and for forty years he taught.

E. And it has been taught on Tannaite authority: Forty years before the destruction of the Temple the sanhedrin went into exile and conducted its sessions in Hanut.

F. And said R. Isaac bar Abodimi, "That is to say that the sanhedrin did not judge cases involving penalties."

G. Do you think it was cases involving penalties? [Such cases were not limited to the sanhedrin but could be tried anywhere in the Land of Israel!]

H. Rather, the sanhedrin did not try capital cases.

I. And we have learned in the Mishnah:

J. After the destruction of the house of the sanctuary, Rabban Yohanan b. Zakkai ordained ... [M. R.H. 4:1]. [So the final forty years encompassed the period after the destruction of the Temple, and Yohanan could not, therefore, have served on a sanhedrin that tried capital cases.]

K. Accordingly, at hand is some other Ben Zakkai [than Yohanan b. Zakkai].

L. That conclusion, moreover, is reasonable, for if you think that it is Rabban Yohanan ben Zakkai, would Rabbi [in the Mishnah-passage] have called him merely, "Ben Zakkai"? [Not very likely.]

M. And lo, it has been taught on Tannaite authority:

N. There is the precedent that Rabban Yohanan ben Zakkai conducted an interrogation about the stalks on the figs [so surely this is the same figure as at M. 5:2B].

O. But [at the time at which the incident took place, capital cases were tried by the sanhedrin and] he was a disciple in session before his master. He said something, and the others found his reasoning persuasive, [41B] so they adopted [the ruling] in his name.

P. When he was studying Torah, therefore, he was called Ben Zakkai, as a disciple in session before his master, but when he [later on] taught, he was called Rabban Yohanan ben Zakkai.

Q. When, therefore, he is referred to as Ben Zakkai, it is on account of his being a beginning [student] and when he is called Rabban Yohanan b. Zakkai, it is on account of his status later on.

Before explaining the relevance, to Schiffman's work, of the Talmudic passage, let us see how the argument from contents works elsewhere.

Modernist scholars have claimed to explain diverse versions of a single saying or story by much the same thesis as we see before us. That is to say, they alleged that they know why a given detail is added here, dropped there, changed in the third place, built up and augmented in the fourth, and on and on. Accordingly, the modern, critical scholars accomplish a kind of incremental history. This is the history of what happened to account for changes in versions of a story, based on a theory of what might have impelled an author to add or revise a given detail. Indeed, practitioners of the incremental approach have not hesitated to declare that they know an entire history for which the text at hand supplies no evidence whatsoever. They then refer to this (entirely undocumented) history in order to explain shifts and changes in versions of a story. All of this rests solely on the contents of what is said, and that is the main point.

This attitude typifies a broader trend toward retrograde analysis, it is the *it-stands-to-reason* and the *contents-of-the-source-indicate*-school of critical scholarship. A fine example is supplied by David J. Halperin, *The Merkabah in Rabbinic Literature* (New Haven, 1980: American Oriental Series 62). Halperin refers to the Merkavah-materials. He posits that, prior to the first written version there was an entire cycle of such stories ("presumably oral"!). He knows that one of these stories had a narrative framework, then lost a miraculous element, then got that miracle reinserted later on. This literary history, claiming to explain shifts and changes in the sequence of stories we saw earlier, derives from not a shred of evidence of any kind. Halperin introduces appropriate qualifications and caveats. But he pays little attention to them; they are mainly formalities. Here is how he states his conclusions (pp. 138-9):

1. I postulate the following development for the merkabah tradition involving R. Johanan b. Zakkai: (1) A cycle of merkabah stories, presumably oral, recounted the miracles that accompanied the expositions of one or another of R. Johanan's disciples; the stories of this cycle contained little beside the miracles. (This stage is purely hypothetical, and is not attested by any literary source.) (2) One of these stories, which involved R. Eleazar b. Arakh, was given a narrative framework, which suggested that R. Eleazar exemplified the "scholar" of M. Hag. 2:1 (Mek. Rashbi). (3) The miraculous element was "censored" from the story of R. Eleazar, possibly by the compiler of the mystical collection (Tosefta). (4) Miraculous details were reinserted, and stories of other disciples added, on the basis of the old merkabah stories (PT, BT)....

3. If my hypothesis is correct, the merkabah tradition is rooted in a cycle of miraculous legends. Some historical reality may hide behind these legends, but it is nearly inaccessible. Instead of trying to recover it, we should focus on what the legends can teach us about (maaseh) merkabah and the image of those reported to have been expert in it.

Halperin's exposition of his own theories omits all reference to whatever he holds as a basic thesis on the character of the literature and its formation, if any. Yet even on the surface, it is clear, he proposes to make up explanations for diverse versions of the Merkavah-story. Each detail has its day. Like others of the younger generation Halperin inserts the marks of a critical approach; all the required language is there. But his premise remains what it is. No detail escapes Halperin's imaginative reconstruction of its individual life-history. Everything means something somewhere -- and to Halperin it does not matter where. It follows that the theory of "incremental history," inventing and then assigning a particular event or motive or other explanation for each change in a story as it moves from document to document finds exemplification in Halperin's treatment of the Merkavah-story. All of this, I repeat, rests solely on the contents of the passage. There is not a shred of critical analysis of literary problems. In the end the court of appeal is to nothing other than the contents of the story.

That brings us to Lawrence H. Schiffman, *Who Was a Jew? Rabbinic and Halakhic Perspectives on the Jewish-Christian Schism* (Hoboken, 1985: Ktav Publishing House, Inc.), pp. 19-20, 27-30, who, on pp. 19-20, states:

> Since Second Temple times, there have been four basic requirements for conversion to Judaism: (1) acceptance of the Torah, (2) circumcision for males, (3) immersion, and (4) sacrifice (no longer required after the destruction).
>
> These requisites are explained in a statement attributed to Rabbi Judah the Prince in Sifre Be-Midbar 108:
>
> > Rabbi says: Just as Israel did not enter the covenant except by means of three things -- circumcision, immersion, and the acceptance of a sacrifice -- so it is the same with the proselytes.
>
> This statement is based on a series of 'aggadot to the effect that Israel was circumcised shortly before the eating of the first paschal lamb, was immersed, and offered sacrifices in preparation for the giving of the Torah at Mount Sinai. Rabbi Judah the Prince understands the entire conversion procedure as an opportunity for the proselyte to celebrate his own reception of the Torah as Israel did at Mount Sinai, for only through sharing in this historic religious experience could the convert become a Jew.
>
> The conversion procedure and ceremony is described in a long baraita' in B. Yevamot 47a-b:
>
> > Our Rabbis taught: A proselyte who comes to convert at this time, we say to him: "Why did you decide to convert? Do you not know that Israel at this time is afflicted, oppressed, downtrodden, and rejected, and that tribulations are visited upon them?" If he says, "I am aware, but I am unworthy," we accept him immediately, and we make known to him a few of the lighter commandments and a few of the weightier commandments, and we make known to him the penalty for transgression of gleaning (the poor man's share), the forgotten (sheaves), the corner, and the poor man's tithe. And we make known to him the punishment for violating the commandments. ... And just as we make known to him the punishment for violating the commandments, so we also make known to him the reward for their observance. ... We are not too lengthy with him nor are we too detailed. If he accepts (this), we circumcise him immediately. ... Once he has recovered, we immerse him immediately. And two scholars stand over him and make known to him some of the lighter and some of the weightier commandments. If he immersed validly, he is like an Israelite in all matters. (In the case of) a woman, women position her in the water up to her neck, and two scholars stand outside and make known to her some of the lighter commandments and some of the weightier commandments. ...
>
> *From the language of our baraita', with its stress on the persecution and downtrodden nature of Israel, it is most likely to have been composed in its present form in the aftermath of either the Great Revolt of 66-784 C.E. or the Bar Kokhba Revolt (132-35 C.E.).*

The passage I have italicized makes the point. The language permits us to date the passage, pure and simple. Since the language says thus and so, the passage *is most likely to have been composed in its present form....* This, I submit, represents a premise no different from the one we saw in connection with ben Zakkai/Yohanan ben Zakkai. The language on its own tells us facts. Without attention to the document that presents the language, the context of that document, or any other variables, and a person can think of many, Schiffman adduces in evidence for the facts at hand merely what the text alleges -- that alone. I do not exaggerate the matter, since Schiffman is clear in claiming: "composed in its present form." He proceeds to state:

> Regardless of which of these two dates is correct, the baraita' reflects the legal rulings prevalent among the tannaim by the Yavnean period, as will be seen below. That the baraita' does not represent the procedure as followed before 70 C.E. is certain from the absence of mention of the sacrifice which would have been included had the Temple cult still been functioning.

This argument appeals to what the passage says, and does not say, as evidence for the facts of the matter. Nor does Schiffman leave himself room for maneuver. He states simply, "...is certain from the absence of mention...." He tells us that, from the content of the passage, we can learn the facts of the matter -- and that without regard to a single question of critical importance.

Schiffman could not have written this book without the principle I have shown he invokes. Let us proceed to another instance. On pp. 27-30 Schiffman says the following:

> M. Pesahim 8:8 has been cited as evidence that immersion of proselytes was already practiced in the late first century B.C.E., even before the destruction:
>
>> If a proselyte converted on the day before Passover, the House of Shammai says: He immerses and eats his paschal offering in the evening. But the House of Hillel says: One who departs from (his) foreskin is (as impure) as one who departs from a grave.
>
> This mishnah concerns a convert who was circumcised on the fourteenth of Nisan, the day on which the paschal sacrifice is slaughtered. The House of Shammai says that he is to immerse that day and to eat the paschal sacrifice in the evening. The House of Hillel says that this proselyte should be considered at least as impure as one who had been at a grave and who therefore had contracted the impurity of the dead (cf. Num. 19:18f.). This would mean that following the completion of the conversion (including the immersion), the proselyte would still have to wait seven days and undergo the required ablutions to be cleansed of the impurity of the dead. B. Pesahim 92a explains this as a Rabbinic ordinance designed to ensure that the new Jew would not err in future years by thinking that he could purify himself from impurity of the dead in the morning before coming to the Temple and partake of the paschal sacrifice that same evening. A passage in T. Pesahim 7:14 supports this interpretation:
>
>> Said Rabbi Eleazar, son of Rabbi Zadok: The House of Shammai and the House of Hillel (both) agree that an uncircumcised male (Jew) receives sprinkling and then eats. Concerning what do they disagree? Regarding an uncircumcised non-Jew. For the House of Shammai says:

> He immerses and then eats his paschal offering in the evening. But the House of Hillel says: One who departs from (his) foreskin is (as impure) as one who departs from a grave. The law is the same for the non-Jew who was circumcised and the female slave who immersed. Rabbi Eliezer ben Jacob says: There were soldiers and gatekeepers in Jerusalem who immersed and ate their paschal offerings in the evening.

Schiffman cites the foregoing out of its context, so he does not tell us that it forms part of a sequence of interpretations of what was originally at issue between the houses. What we have is only one possibility among a number of proposals. For Schiffman it is definitive.

> Rabbi Eleazar ben Zadok explains that all agree that in a case in which a Jew is circumcised on the day before Passover, he may be sprinkled in advance. After circumcision, as is known from parallels, he immerses and then may eat of the paschal offering. The disagreement in our mishnah, the Tosefta tells us, concerns only a non-Jew who was circumcised on the day before Passover. The House of Shammai allows him to eat of the paschal offering immediately after his immersion. The House of Hillel regards him as being as impure as if he had contracted the impurity of the dead. He must, therefore, wait the seven-day purification period to be cleansed of impurity of the dead. This is in order to be certain that he will not err in future years and partake of the paschal offering or visit the Temple while in a state of impurity. So the House of Hillel actually required two ablutions, one for conversion and one for purification, while the House of Shammai required only one.
>
> The Tosefta then notes that the House of Hillel takes the same view regarding a handmaiden who has immersed. In order for her to partake of the paschal offering, she must be purified as if she had contracted impurity of the dead.
>
> Finally, to illustrate the view of the Shammaites, Rabbi Eliezer ben Jacob relates that there were Roman soldiers and gatekeepers in Jerusalem who converted and were allowed to eat of the paschal offering after immersion without purification from impurity of the dead. There is no further evidence as to why these Roman soldiers would have decided to convert at the last minute. One may speculate, however, that the pageantry and beauty of the preparations for the paschal sacrifice and the Passover festival enticed them to enter into the jewish people so as to be able to participate.

Here again, I stop to point out that Schiffman takes for granted the historicity of the allegation about the Roman soldiers and gatekeepers. Since it is a fact, we can hasten on to add "critical" speculation on why the soldiers converted at the last minute, though we can speculate, etc. etc. etc. The speculation about why the people did what they did underlines the simple credulity at hand. Since the source at hand says the soldiers did it, they did it, and our problem is to ask why.

> This material has been treated at length here in order to clarify a passage which has been treated facilely in some discussions of conversion. It is certain that when the Mishnah and Tosefta refer to immersion here, this is the immersion which was part of the conversion ceremony. When the tannaim wanted to designate the

purification from the impurity of the dead which is also required by the Hillelites, it is referred to as sprinkling. It can be stated with certainty, then, that our passage assumes the requirements of immersion for conversion.

And again:

> How precisely can we date this material? First, the Mishnah and Tosefta concern a dispute of the houses of Hillel and Shammai which must have taken place either while the Temple still stood or in the early Yavnean period. By this time, there is no disagreement at all about the requirement of immersion. Different versions of the baraita' place the explanation in the name of Rabbi Eleazar ben Zadok, Rabbi Yose ben Judah, and Rabbi Simeon ben Eleazar. There were two tannaim named Eleazar ben Zadok. It is probable that we are dealing here with the latter. Nonetheless, it should be remembered that he lived during the Temple period and related things about the Temple in his teachings. Rabbi Yose ben Judah is a contemporary of Rabbi Judah the Prince, redactor of the Mishnah. The statement also appears in B. Pesahim 92a in the name of Rabbi Simeon ben Eleazar, a pupil of Rabbi Meir and contemporary of Judah the Prince.

Once more we find ourselves in the world where a source must not merely refer to, but derive from, the time at which Yohanan was young, because it calls him ben Zakkai, and the other version derives from the time at which he had risen to power, because it gives him his title.

What is wrong here is not that Schiffman cannot be right. It is that he has no way of telling whether he is wrong, therefore of testing, and permitting others to test, the validity of his proposition. I point to the simple fact that Schiffman here does take for granted Eleazar ben Zadok really said what is assigned to him, at the time the Temple stood, no less, so we now have a fact about the state of the halakhah in the time of the Temple. The fact that other sources attribute the saying to much later authorities makes no difference; we simply record that fact, without taking it seriously. We have what we want. Schiffman argues as follows:

> On the one hand, we have failed to establish a definite attestation of our tradition at an early date. *On the other hand, the transmission of this statement in the names of three separate tannaim indicates that it was widespread, and we may therefore take it as reliable evidence that the dispute of the Hillelites and Shammaites circulated from the Yavnean period on in the schools of the tannaim* [italics mine].

To three different names the saying is imputed, so Schiffman concludes that it was widespread. Schiffman is not alone in equating recurrence of a story with circulation of that story; others we shall shortly read will draw the conclusion that the event portrayed by the story happened very often. That is an undoubted fact. But so what? We may therefore take it as reliable evidence. Once more, true. But evidence as to what? What is the force of the *therefore* ?

The only reliable evidence I see is that the same saying is imputed to three names. I do not know what, on that basis, the dispute circulated broadly or circulated at all. Nothing in hand even pertains to that matter. We know only that the same thing is assigned to three names, and that proves, on the face of it, that no one was sure who said what. That does not seem to me reliable evidence of any proposition except one: people were confused. Just because different sources say different people made the same statement, we cannot imagine that a lot of people said the same thing -- except in the never-never-land of Talmudic history, Talmud-style.

Let us hear Schiffman's conclusions, on the basis of the passage at hand and in direct sequence from the foregoing:

> What can now be said about the evidence for the dating of immersion as a requirement for conversion? First, it seems that it is necessary to date it before the time of John the Baptist and the rise of Christianity in order to understand the background against which baptism comes to the fore. Second, tannaitic evidence, although admittedly lacking early attestation, also lends support to the claim that immersion was already a necessary requirement for conversion in late Second Temple times. Nonetheless, we cannot prove that immersion was a sine qua non for conversion before the early first century C.E.

Schiffman is satisfied that he has made his point. He invokes an entirely critical, contemporary rhetoric. He claims this: baptism was required by *the halakhah* in particular in the last century before the destruction. Schiffman admits he cannot prove baptism was required *before* that time. But the proof that it was required in "the halakhah" in the period before 70 rests on our accepting as fact one among several attributions of rules maintaining that immersion is necessary. If the cited rabbi really made the statement, then we know as fact that that rabbi held that opinion -- no more than that.

v

Example of Gullibility as Historical and Methodological Naivete: Steven T. Katz on Yavneh and Herbert Basser on "the Pharisaic Idea of Law as a Sacred Cosmos"

Steven T. Katz, "Issues in the Separation of Judaism and Christianity after 70 C.E.: A Reconsideration," *Journal of Biblical Literature* 103, 1984, pp. 43-76 provides a fine example of historical naiveté, and Herbert Basser, "The Development of the Pharisaic Idea of Law as a Sacred Cosmos," *Journal for the Study of Judaism* 16, 1984, pp. 104-115, of methodological insufficiency. On pp. 46-7 of his article, Katz states:

> In addition, the leading Palestinian Tannaim were frequent travelers. The Talmud records a journey of R. Gamaliel, R. Eliezer ben Azariah, R. Akiba, and R.

Joshua to Rome, as well as the travels of many other sages throughout Palestine and its environs and also to Babylonia and points west.

Katz's footnote is not to a source at all, but to W. D. Davies, *Setting of the Sermon on the Mount* , pp. 295-6. So we do not know how Katz proposes to read the stories about the "leading Tannaim" as "frequent travelers." We do not know what sources Katz has in mind. The "frequent travels" may in fact be the same story told a number of times. But, it is clear, Katz does believe these trips took place . Without further discussion of why he thinks so, he presents us with just another example of gullibility. He does not know the rather sizable literature on the stories, going back three quarters of a century. Katz, not knowing or even resorting to the sources, can tell us what the rabbis had to say on their "historical" journeys:

> No doubt during such travels the criticism of Jewish Christianity voiced at Yavneh was discussed and propagated among the Jewish communities of the Diaspora.

But why no doubt? How does Katz know? He does not let us in on his secret.

> Further, there is no reason to doubt that much unofficial decrying of Jesus and Christianity occurred orally.

How does Katz know this? What evidence does he have of the folk oral tradition? How does he know that *Toledot Yeshu* goes back (the gist? the wording too?) to the period at hand?. Very soon the "no doubt" and "no reason to doubt" turns into a fact. Here is how an "it would not be surprising," one sentence later turns into a fact:

> It would also not be surprising if the folk, oral tradition, which was later embellished and codified as the Toledot Yeshu, also had its start in these circumstances. If Jews were to accept the Christian account of the virgin birth or the resurrection they would be on their way to becoming Christians. From the Jewish perspective such claims were "unbelievable" and thus open to caricature and lampooning. However, it needs to be emphasized that vulgar and popular criticism, while not surprising, should not be confused with any "official" letter of condemnation from Yavneh or elsewhere. For the latter there is no evidence in rabbinic sources.

What is at stake for Katz? He wants to oppose the views that the Jews told really nasty stories about Jesus. Here is what he says:

> The excesses of Harnack, repeated most recently by Frend, concerning the nature of 'official' Jewish communications, compared with casual, if negative, 'gossip, need to be noted if only to be rejected as unfounded.

Katz appears to be saying: Harnack and Frend hold that there were official Jewish *communications*. But Katz holds there was only casual, if negative, *gossip*. I am not sure why Katz thinks this makes things nice. If this is his sense, then Katz believes the story that rabbis made trips. He wants to turn these trips into something other than propaganda missions, organized to oppose Christianity. How does he do it? It is enchanting: with a few well placed "no doubts" and "there is no reason to doubt" and "it would also not be surprising," Katz has invented not only the subject matter of the rabbis' discourse with the Jews in distant places but the exact content. He knows what they told the other Jews, and he even tells us that the Jews found these beliefs "unbelievable," thus open to caricature and lampooning. He does not have a footnote to point to first century evidence of this kind of caricature and lampooning. But he knows that it was vulgar and popular criticism. Then he has told us that it would not be surprising of the sages at hand told nasty stories when they made their trip. But this is not really "official" and it is only casual. But that makes it nice, or, at least, nicer.

Not a single primary source is cited, let alone analyzed. The entire vision derives from Katz's arguments from, and with, secondary scholarship. The argument at hand is based on what is mostly Katz's own doctrine of what the rabbis said on their frequent travels.

Basser's article concerns the historical Pharisees. But he wishes to argue with a number of scholars (generally not specified by name). He has his views of who the Pharisees were and what he thinks is important about them.[1] Basser's basic polemic about the historical Pharisees appears to be as follows:

> The assertion that Judaism was fossilized by Pharisaic doctrine did not withstand the test of scholarly investigation. Others became so involved in apologetics that they lost sight of the spiritual, numinous and mystic impact with which the Pharisees made law into religion, not religion into law.

---

[1]Here is what Basser has to say, on pp. 104-105 of his article:

A considerable number of scholars have examined the rise and success of the Pharisees.

At this point Basser gives us the following footnote:

> See Bibliography to 'Pharisees' in *Encyclopaedia Judaica*. ..; also Finkelstein, L. *The Pharisees*....; Moore, G.F., *Judaism in the First Centuries of the Christian Era*.. ..; Schuerer, E., *A History of the Jewish People in the Time of Jesus* (New York, 1961); Tcherikover, V., *Hellenistic Civilization and the Jews* , Jerusalem, 1959; Gibbon, E., *Decline and Fall of the Roman Empire,* London, 1795.

To list what Basser chooses not to mention on a subject much debated would take many pages. But the resort to Finkelstein, a generation ago, Moore, two generations ago, Schuerer, four generations ago, and then, in a grand leap, all the way back to none other than Gibbon, 1795! -- that is either a joke of remarkable subtlety or a statement of sheer indifference to learning. " I express astonishment at the *Journal for the Study of Judaism* for printing an article that exhibits utter ignorance of scholarship since, if not 1795, then, at least, 1971.

I genuinely find puzzling what he means by Pharisaism, Pharisees, and Pharisaic doctrine. What sources does he identify as Pharisaic, and how does he know what the Pharisees (before 70? after 70?) thought or did not think? He does not tell us. He plunges ahead, taking up a polemic lacking all focus and purpose. He speaks of "the assertion," but we do not know whose assertion or with whom he argues. Then comes his "others," who did something I cannot quite get straight. I do not know who Basser's "others are." But I also cannot tell why he is angry with them.

And what burden Basser proposes to bear against his foes I cannot report. For I do not understand what he means when he says, they "became so involved in apologetics that they lost sight of the spiritual, numinous, and mystic impact with which the Pharisees made law into religion, not religion into law." I cite some more of his statement:

> Certain philosophical and methodological stumbling blocks may account for some common oversights. Scholars of the previous generation traced the evolution of primitive Semitic notions. These primitive ideas were said to have slowly evolved into the highest achievement of the Israelite prophets. They considered the moral grandeur of the prophets to be unparalleled in religious history. The recurrence of a purely moral and ethical religion has been hampered by our continuing to use Stoical allegories to interpret Scripture. These methods force the 'primitive' Bible to yield all desired truths while obscuring the lofty ideals of morality. Christianity is nothing but Hellenized Judaism while Judaism itself assimilated ancient superstition and remains unchanged since the days of the New Testament. They were concerned that the future of religious evolution may end in the practice of morality made easier by the use of theological symbols. Some scholars indeed, posited that the Pharisees had accomplished this task. But in succeeding generations these symbols were treated as real existences, as dogmatic idols.

> Envelloped [sic] by the ideals of 'Christian Humanism' or 'Prophetic Judaism', they found 'ethics' to be a final stage of religious evolution.

> Their historical studies foundered somewhat also. Usually the activities of an obscure period of religion prior to the obscure period to its state after the period, we can ascertain what must have occurred. Names of groups that trace their origin to the obscure period often contain clues to the nature of the period and the groups. Folk histories may possess kernels of truth that shed light on the times.

> However, these categories have not proved successful in the attempt to determine the origin and activities of the Pharisees. Change is difficult to measure because we have little idea of the Persian period which preceded the rise of the Pharisees. Even the term 'Pharisee' remains ambiguous with 'separatists', 'puritans' and 'interpreters' all given as possible meanings. Rabbinic writings pose difficulties. The Rabbis did not consider the Pharisees as a new group but as the successors of the prophets. For them Moses and the Israelites were followers of Pharisaism even if they did not use the term. They referred to Moses as 'our Rabbi' completely blurring any distinction in the Judaism of the Bible and that of their own day. But it is just here, in the beliefs, practices and struggles of the Rabbis that we can distill the development of Pharisaic doctrine. The works of non-Palestinians like Philo and the writings of Palestinians such as Josephus and the

Qumran scrolls allow us to appreciate the faithfulness of the Rabbis to Pharisaic tradition. Finally, the very keen insights of the medieval rabbis are indispensable in appreciating the labors of the Pharisees.

In his celebrated disputation, Nachmanides claimed that the Jews were experts in the theory of religion. Perhaps he meant that when the early Pharisees faced the task of strengthening Judaism to withstand Hellenism, they formulated conceptions concerning the behavior of religious beliefs in changing environments. In fact, they did develop naive but penetrating theories of history and the psychology of religion. They prescribed Torah study, ritual observance, charity, and separateness as the key to religious preservation. If Nachmanides referred to these theories, he was indeed accurate in his assertion.

The reader will not be surprised to learn that the statements at hand refer to not a single specific text or scholarly monograph. It is all run-on, without one footnote.

vi

Example of Gullibility as Neglect of Sources: Harvey Falk on Jesus the Pharisee (!)

Harvey Falk, *Jesus the Pharisee. A New Look at the Jewishness of Jesus* (New York & Mahwah, 1985: Paulist Press) wishes to prove that Jesus was a Pharisee of the House of Hillel and he was betrayed by the House of Shammai. While Falk thinks he is telling us things that happened in the first century, he found all this out in a letter published by Rabbi Jacob Emden to the Polish rabbinate concerning early Christianity. Emden published the letter in 1757. Falk has discovered Emden and proposes to resurrect Emden's thesis.

Falk does not devote a single chapter of his book to Jesus. He does not deal with a single work of New Testament scholarship. He quotes his proof-texts from the New Testament without a shred of analysis. In point of fact he does not commonly quote New Testament passages, he merely alludes to them. They nonetheless supply facts, just as the Talmudic literature provides him with facts. These are his chapter-headings: *Rabbi Jacob Emden's views on Christianity; Hillel's convert revisited, a second look; Talmud and Jewish tradition on the Essenes; relationship of the Essenes to Bet [House of] Hillel; the arrest of Rabbi Eliezer and its relationship to the beliefs of the minim (Jewish Christians); Hasidim of the nations, Parallel definitions; the relationship of Rabbi Eliezer to the School of Shammai; the roots of Christian anti-Semitism: Bet Hillel vs. Bet Shammai; understanding the Christian Bible through Bet Shammai and Bet Hillel.* While the New Testament is cited, as are talmudic documents, chapter and verse, not a single passage is subjected to close analysis in a chapter or even in a paragraph. In point of fact Falk takes at face value everything he finds everywhere. Falk's list of modern scholars contains the name of not a single New Testament scholar.

Rather than further cataloguing the traits of the book, let us turn directly to Falk's own words. On pp. 30-31 he states:

A MISSION TO THE GENTILES BY THE HASIDIM

Although Judaism never attempted to missionize for converts to its religion, the discussion of the Talmud (Sanhedrin 57a) and especially Maimonides (Melakhim, Chap. 8) would seem to indicate that Moses obligated the Jews to spread knowledge of the Noahide commandments to all mankind. It is surprising, then, that no historical record exists recording such an endeavor. Especially in ancient times, when the world was mired in pagan and barbaric beliefs, one would have expected such a movement.

For the uninitiated, Maimonides is not the same as the Talmud, but Falk routinely invokes medieval commentaries to testify about the state of affairs in the first century.

I have previously presented Rabbi Jacob Emden's view (Sefer Shimmush and Appendix to Seder Olam) that the original intent of Jesus and Paul was to bring the seven Noahide commandments to the Gentiles, while the Jews should continue their adherence to Judaism. His view is generally unknown outside scholarly circles, although it is recorded in the three major Jewish encyclopedias (Universal Jewish Encyclopaedia 3:190, Jewish Encyclopedia 5:623, and Judaica 3:198).

References to this "original intent" of both Jesus and Paul (no less) to bring the seven Noahide commandments to the gentiles do not include attention to the sources, only to secondary literature, faithfully cited, volume and page. How do we know what Jesus and Paul originally intended? What sources does Falk adduce in evidence? I see only references to three major Jewish encyclopaedias.

It might be mentioned here that most scholars have rejected R. Emden's stance. Nor is it my intention here to discuss the pros and cons of his positive views on the founders of Christianity, as Jews are traditionally reticent to discuss other religions, and especially Christianity. But considering the extreme puzzles associated with the Dead Sea Scrolls, and specifically the evidence that Jesus and Paul were acquainted with the Qumran sect -- as many phrases from the Christian Bible seem to have been borrowed from the older Scrolls -- I would wonder whether R. Emden's thesis might not serve as a key to unravel the mystery.

The majority of the scholarly community agrees that the Qumran sect were members of the Essenes (also known as Hasidim or Tze'nuim in Talmudic literature). No doubt can be entertained that the Essenes were extremely observant of the halakha, and no evidence of basic Christological beliefs has been found in the Scrolls.

How does Falk know that the Essenes of Qumran are identical with the Hasidim and the like in Talmudic literature? I find no footnote on the page at hand. It may be so, it may not be so. That is not at issue. What is at issue is how we know what we claim to have happened. While the Essenes had law, no one has succeeded in showing that their laws were the same as those of the rabbis, though there are points of intersection. On the contrary, the notions that there was a single *halakhah*, that at Qumran the halakhah now represented in the rabbinic literature prevailed, and equivalent views enjoy no proof whatever. Falk thinks them plausible or obvious, so they must be so. He goes on:

> Wouldn't it therefore be quite logical to assume that the opening paragraph of the Manual of Discipline, giving the raison d'être of the sect as "to do what is good and upright ... as He has commanded through Moses," would also include spreading the knowledge of the Noahide Commandments to the Gentiles, as commanded by Moses? And when they further wrote "to love all the sons of light ..." wouldn't that have included Gentiles who observed the Noahide Laws? I am not, however, insinuating that Jesus or Paul acted directly in collaboration with the Essenes or any other body.

> In his letter to the Council of the Four Lands, Rabbi Emden, in what might be construed as a prophetic statement by a German rabbi rather than a literary slip, urges Christians to help Jews observe the Torah, as "commanded to you by your first teachers." He does not mention the names of Jesus and Paul here, but goes on to assure Christians that doing so will bring them reward and blessing. Could this rabbinic giant have sensed -- two hundred years prior to the discovery of the Scrolls -- that a group of pious Jews some two thousand years ago had sought to help their brethren observe the Torah during the coming exile by making Gentiles aware of its eternal binding character upon the Israelites?

The argument by the asking of questions speaks for itself. Let us move on to another sustained passage, so we may taste the full flavor of Falk's book. The following appears on pp. 49-51. I shall refrain from interrupting:

> A Mission to the Gentiles by the Essenes and Bet Hillel

> Talmud, Sukkah 28A: "Hillel the Elder had 80 disciples, 30 of whom were worthy of the Divine Spirit resting upon them ... 30 of whom were worthy that the sun should stand still for them ... The greatest of them was Jonathan ben Uzziel, the smallest of them was Johanan ben Zakkai ..."

> Jerusalem Talmud (Nedarim, end Ch. 5): "Hillel the Elder had 80 pairs of disciples ..."

> Question: Why was R. Johanan ben Zakkai appointed Nasi -- rather than one of the other 79, who were greater than he? And what became of the remaining 79?

> Question: There seems to be a conflict here between the Babylonian and Jerusalem Talmuds as to whether Hillel had 80 or 160 disciples!

> For a proper reply to these queries, I believe we must turn to Hagigah 16A, where the Mishnah speaks of the first dispute that arose among the sages of Israel: it deals with the issue of whether the laying on of hands (on the head of sacrifice) was permitted on a festival. Four succeeding pairs of Nasi (President of the Sanhedrin) and Av-Bet-Din (Vice-President of the Sanhedrin) disagreed, but Hillel and Menahem did not differ. Menahem went forth, Shammai entered (in his place). Hillel and Shammai then disagreed.

R. Jehiel Heilprin (Seder Ha-Dorot 2:271) identifies this Menahem, who first served with Hillel, as Menahem the Essene -- whom Herod was fond of for having prophesied his rise to power. Such modern scholars as Kaufmann Kohler and Louis Ginzberg agreed with this identification.

The Talmud to this Mishnah asks what actually happened to Menahem. Abbaye and Rava -- two Amoraim who lived during the fourth century C.E. -- disagreed concerning this. Abbaye claimed that Menahem went forth into evil ways; Rava states he went forth to the King's service. The Talmud brings a baraita to support Rava's view, where it is stated that Menahem went forth to the King's service, along with 80 pairs of disciples dressed in silk.

This dispute among the later Talmudic authorities over what happened to Menahem -- probably about 20 B.C.E. -- is also cited in the Jerusalem Talmud (Hagigah 2:2), albeit anonymously and with added detail. The first opinion describes Menahem as having left the Pharisees to join a conflicting religious group (the Essenes), which only reiterates Abbaye's negative stance toward Menahem -- and the Essenes as well. To Rava's view is added a postscript explaining that Menahem was forced to leave because the Gentiles were coercing (or would soon coerce?) the Jews to abandon their religious beliefs, and he and the 80 pairs of disciples left to remedy this. Rava thus adopts a positive view of Menahem's departure, which according to R. David Fraenkel (Karban ha-Edah), was a mission to reconcile or appease "the nations." (It should be noted here that in scores of disputes between Rava and Abbaye in the Talmud, the view of the former is always -- with six specific exceptions -- accepted.)

We of course recognize that we are dealing here with an historic-philosophic dispute between Rava and Abbaye, and not one concerning a specific halakha. Also, Rava's statement concerning achieving a reconciliation with the Gentiles calls for further elucidation, as we do not recall mention of such a mission elsewhere.

Returning now to the Baraita of R. Phineas ben Jair mentioned at the beginning of this chapter, we recall that Hasidism was listed as a higher degree of spiritual attainment than Pharisaism; yet the sources would seem to indicate that most Talmudic sages did not practice Hasidism -- whether on an individual basis or in an organized state, such as the Essenes did. R. Moshe Hayyim Luzzatto, in his classic, Mesillat Yesharim (Ch. 13), explains that both Pharisaism and Hasidism involve observance of the Torah beyond the letter of the law, and Pharisaism is also referred to as "Mishnah of the Hasidim," praised by the Prophet Elijah. However, while Pharisaism in the main denotes abstinence and "building fences," which is the first phase of Hasidism, Hasidism itself demands more positive action. We might also note here that Rava is mentioned several times by Luzzatto as one who practiced Hasidism.

Abbaye's negative outlook toward the Essenes and Hasidism might be understood in light of his remark (Berakhot 45A), "Go forth and see how the public are accustomed to act," in concert with Hillel's statement, "An ignorant man cannot be a Hasid" (Avot 2:5). In other words, some religious leaders feared that Hasidism might cause a schism between the laity and the scholarly community. But Luzzatto cites an even greater danger inherent in Hasidism (Ch. 20) -- namely, that an action in itself may seem worthy enough of performance, but the results might prove harmful. He cites two examples. Gedaliah ben Ahikam, appointed Governor of Judah by the Babylonians, who -- because of his Hasidism -- refused to accept Johanan ben Kareach's warning concerning Ishmael ben Nathaniah's treacherous intentions (Jeremiah 40). As a result, Gedaliah was killed, the Jews' last hopes for independence at the time were dashed, and Jeremiah considered Gedaliah personally responsible for those murdered by Ishmael. Luzzatto cites as another example the Talmud's condemnation of R. Zechariah ben Avkulot (Gittin 56A), whose act of Hasidism led to the Second Temple's destruction. This is surely why Abbaye and many others shunned (and deprecated) acts of Hasidism which might ultimately cause harm to the people.

If we take for granted that whatever is attributed to a rabbi really was said by him, we end up in the fantasy-world constructed by Falk, a world in which if we ask a question, through what seems "logical" or self-evident, we answer it and so create a fact. No evidence, no analysis of sources, no differentiation among earlier late or medieval sources, no recognition that eighteenth century rabbis were no more present in the first century than was George Washington -- none of these simple and obvious traits of mind characterize Falk in these passages. True, Falk is an Orthodox rabbi. But he claims to have an opinion we can subject to rational discourse. Otherwise (to argue in his way) why publish this book? And (to indulge ourselves in this wonderfully pleasing mode of proving a case, the asking of questions bearing self-evident answers) why should his Orthodoxy relieve him from the duty of constructing an intelligible argument? Since he writes for the twenty-first century, he has the obligation to speak in the language of the present, not to compose arguments consisting of rhetorical questions, on the one side, or medieval syllogisms, propositions proved by a peculiar, deductive logic, on the other.

vii
An Israeli Voice: Pinchas Pelli's Assumption

We turn aside to listen to an Israeli, but one who addresses the West in English and in a reputable scholarly journal. Pinchas Hacohen Pelli, "The Havurot That Were in Jerusalem," *Hebrew Union College Annual* 55, 1984, pp. 55-74, cites à statement of Eleazar b. R. Sadoq about societies in Jerusalem in the time of the Temple. What is important for our purpose is the reason that he offers for believing (1) that Eleazar made the stated attributed to him, and (2) that Eleazar is right. It is fair to address these questions to him, because he explicitly says, "Is his statement to be taken as actual fact about specific societies that existed in Jerusalem?" So we have a right to ask how he proposes to answer this question. His first problem is simple. There are two authorities by the same name, so Pelli asks which of the two speaks in the cited passage. He states on p. 56:

> We can assume that the transmitter of the above report is R. Eleazar b. R. Zadok
> I, since we do find attributed to him many traditions about life in Jerusalem at the
> time of the Temple.

The assumption rests on the contents of what is said. Why the later Eleazar cannot have made statements about Jerusalem in the time of the Temple I do not know. Pelli does not explain. In fact he begs the question, since what he wants to prove, he posits. He will now proceed to review sayings and stories about the earlier Eleazar. While, quite admirably, he introduces the critical language, *said to have*, the distinction between *did* and *said to have done* makes no difference here. Pelli rapidly slips into the language of historical description. These are things the man really said and did. Thus he writes:

> He was the son of R. Zadok who was said to have fasted forty years that Jerusalem not be destroyed until he fell ill and R. Johanan b. Zakkai turned to Vespasian for a doctor for him. R. Eleazar b. R. Zadok lived another few decades before the Destruction and engaged in commerce with Abba Shaul b. Batnit. He regularly related details of his adventures and of what he saw in Jerusalem before and after the Destruction, and thus, he often tells about the practices of the Jerusalemites. He relates, for example: "we used to leap over coffins containing bodies to see the Israelite kings." He tells of what he himself saw during the period of the Temple: "This was the custom of the men of Jerusalem. When a man left his house he carried his lulav in his hand; when he went to the synagogue his lulav was in his hand, etc." And "Thus did the grocers cry, 'come and buy ingredients for your matza.'" And also, "This is how the scribes in Jerusalem used to make their scrolls." R. Eleazar b. Zadok reports at length, specifically about the practices of the House of Rabban Gamaliel (very often also in the Tosefta), testifying about himself, "I very often ate at Rabban Gamaliel house."

I have not reproduced the individual footnotes joined to these statements. They consist of references to passages of the Babylonian Talmud, the Tosefta, and the like. At no point does Pelli find it necessary to tell us why he believes these stories, what history he finds in their formation, or who he thinks recorded and handed them on, with so remarkably a measure of accuracy, to the much later compilers of the documents in which they are preserved. None of this. If the source -- any source, wherever, whenever compiled and redacted -- says Eleazar said something, he really said it, and if the source says Eleazar did something, he really did it.

> As to time, we can assume, then, that R. Eleazar b. Zadok could give personal and factual testimony about the societies that existed in Jerusalem before the Destruction. He, himself, was active in the city and we have the following: "It is told of R. Eleazar b. Zadok that he purchased the synagogue of the Alexandrians which was in Jerusalem and did therein whatsoever he pleased."
>
> Footnote: 14. *ibid.*, Megillah 3:6. For variants, see Lieberman, Tosefta Kifshutah, Megillah, p.. 1162.

Here Pelli explicitly states that we can assume Eleazar said these things and knew what he was talking about, and the evidence in our hands, at face value, tells us historical facts, pure and simple.

viii

The Pseudocritical Method:
Rosalie Gershenzon and Elieser Slomovic

Let us now turn to the one new development in the past quarter-century:the evasion of the critical problem, along with a claim to have solved it. In their article, "A Second Century Jewish-Gnostic Debate: Rabbi Jose ben Halafta and the Matrona," *Journal for the Study of Judaism* 16, 1984, pp. 1-41, Rosalie Gershenzon and Elieser Slomovic introduce the rhetoric of a critical approach to learning, but not the substance of that approach. In fact they evade the question while pretending to answer it. It is the wave of the future. Let me explain.

Gershenzon and Slomovic carry forward and illustrate the now-familiar gullibility, but their current article advances the discussion. They show most vividly how the younger generation tries to exhibit the stigmata of the critical approach, while, in point of fact, trying to talk their way around it. That is what I would call "pseudocriticism," as I shall explain. But first, let us consider the evidence that they are, in fact, gullible. For otherwise, the charge of pseudocriticism bears no relevance. If they do not pretend to be critical, why accuse them of the pretense? But if they are gullible and then pose as something else, it is another matter. So what makes me classify them with the others? There are two reasons.

First, one mark of gullibility is to translate theological conviction into literary and historical fact. A principal conviction of Judaism is that God revealed one whole Torah, in diverse media, to Moses at Sinai. Consequently, all components of that one whole Torah contribute equally, and with slight differentiation, along with all others. For the fundamentalist historian, the upshot is simple. We ignore the point of origin of all stories and sayings. Anything in the canon bears equal weight with anything else, and that without the slightest regard for the particular document in which a saying or story makes its appearance. The received theology states, "There is no consideration of priority or anachronism in the Torah," and so, for the fundamentalists, the same applies. the two authors cite a broad range of stories about a second century rabbi, in no way, at no point differentiating among those stories by the criterion of their point of documentary origin. For example, they do not tell us that story A appears in a document closed in the second century, story B, in one in the third, story C, in one in the fourth, and so on. Everything is the same as everything else.

Second, the more familiar side of gullibility -- credulity about attributions -- requires only brief restatement. In fairness, I hasten to say they explicitly deny that that is their view. But the two authors insist that all the stories at hand not only speak *about* the second century rabbi but also testify to ideas *held at the time he lived*. The basis for that insistence marks them as fundamentalists. They invoke the contents of the stories to justify the second-century dating of the stories, just like Schiffman. They argue that at the time Yose lived

Gnosticism flourished, so (even though they do not allege he *really* said them) Yose's statements require interpretation in the context of debates between Gnostics and rabbis. But if Yose did not make the sayings attributed to him, then why the second century in particular? We should not have turned to the second century to the exclusion of the third or fourth if the name of Yose did not appear in those sayings -- and if in our mind the appearance of that name did not carry *prima facie* weight that he really made those statements.

The authors go on: in fact, -- so their circular argument goes -- [1] when we read these stories knowing that Yose was arguing with Gnosticism, [2] sure enough, he is arguing with Gnosticism. The fact about Gnosticism is established. But, as I shall ask, is that the only possibility? Where are the others? The two authors do not rigorously examine other possibilities, so they rest their case on the argument from content: it sounds right, so it is right, and the old "ring of truth" sounds loud and clear. We come back to the original observation, that the two authors ignore the time of the appearance of the documents that contain the stories they cite, paying attention only to the contents of the stories but not to their provenance. On that basis, as I said, they immediately leap into the second century -- when Yose lived. So two distinct strands of gullibility intertwine, first, the argument from contents, second, the argument that it does not matter where the saying in his name now is preserved.

Now I wonder, why to begin with should we invoke only second-century Gnosticism in the interpretation of the stories, and ignore whatever other issues or dispute flourished at the time of the composition of the documents that contain the stories? In fact, I have noticed that Genesis Rabbah, universally assigned to the fourth century, contains a systematic refutation of positions we know were held by Gnostics, particularly concerning Creation, the Creator-God, the knowability of the unknown or Most High God, the goodness or evil of Creation, and on and on. Most of these stories, moreover, occur in the name of later third and fourth century authorities. So here we have a quite different setting for a dispute between sages and Gnostics -- after the triumph of Christianity. Now the document at hand may be shown to address issues burning in the Jewish community in particular. It is quite plausible to wonder whether within Jewry people held the positions so vigorously refuted by the exegetes. We are not required therefore to read the stories in relationship to debates between Jews and outsiders. So the second century need not present us with our own hermeneutical option, nor do debates between Jews and gentiles tell us the only setting to which such stories refer. I do not suggest I have proved anything. I mean only to make a simple point.

First, we see an egregious error. The authors ignore the age *in* which the document that contains a story was closed, but immediately introduce the traits of the age *to* which the story refers. Second, the authors announce a thesis but do not test their thesis against contrary possibilities. For the contents of the stories conform to the requirements of their thesis. So here is a fresh and complex version of gullibility, in four aspects: first, second-level gullibility about attributions ("he did not really say it but someone in his day did"), second, indifference to the differentiation among documents and insistence that everything is pretty much the same as everything else, third, appeal to the contents of a story in validation of its historicity (which is the first again), and fourth, failure to validate a theory by constructing a test of falsification.

Now to the evidence, on pp. 1-3 of their article:

> Of the many encounters between Jews and non-Jews recorded in rabbinic literature, surely the most elusive and provocative are the epigrammatic discussions between sages and upper class Roman women during the Imperial Period. In eighteen passages found in various midrashim, R. Jose Ben Halafta, head of the academy in Sepphoris in the second half of the second century C.E., confronts an anonymous "matrona." In the following study, we have identified all of the pertinent passages, and propose to examine the entire corpus afresh, with due attention to its historical and religious background....

So far, so good. The authors take an interest in narrow historical questions. After reviewing earlier approaches and explaining why, in drawing together all of the pertinent passages and treating the whole and not only bits and pieces, they will advance the question, they go on to the critical issue (pp. 2-3):

> Two anticipatory questions arise: can the midrashim in question, embedded in contextual layers which cannot themselves be reliably dated, be ascribed with any certainty to R. Jose? Can the entire polemic be regarded as a historical encounter between two actual antagonists, rather than as a conventional literary vehicle in which the ostensible literary opponent is merely a fiction mouthing widely known arguments?

Here at last is the right question, correctly posed. But wait for the answer. I give it whole and complete, and then come back and analyze its parts:

> After all, many of the questions raised by the matrona were regarded as legitimate exegetical problems within the rabbinic schools. Our proposal that these midrashim be treated as a unit does not depend on a demonstration -- obviously impossible -- that they reflect actual encounters between specific individuals. Whatever the historical and literary impetus for enclosing their contents in this unusual polemical frame work, we believe that they record the major arguments in the second century Gnostic-Jewish debate, as preserved by Jewish spokesmen. Later redactors may no longer have recognized Rabbi Jose's opponent as a Gnostic, but they recognized and preserved the language of religious polemic and the second century Galilean provenance.
>
> There are several a priori reasons for treating this group of midrashim as a unit. First, although a wide variety of encounters between sages and matronas is reported in the literature, both in Palestine and in Rome itself, the passages involving R. Jose are unique. They are the only ones which present a straight forward religious polemic in query-answer format. The polemical approach is

almost invariably exegetical, a pattern which appears to be characteristic of early refutations of heretical doctrine. All the other passages are anecdotal or episodic, and some have cautionary or legendary overtones. Second, the passages under consideration share distinctive features of style and tone, most notably the homely, almost banal illustrations utilized by R. Jose, and the surprisingly friendly mood of the argument. These features will become apparent upon closer acquaintance. Finally, a brief examination of religious, social and political conditions in second century Galilee suggests that at that time and place an encounter between a leading Jewish sage and an educated Roman aristocrat with Gnostic leanings was, if not routine, quite plausible. Indeed, almost no other time and place could have been more suitable. Let us briefly examine some of these contributing factors.

Now let us review these paragraphs. First the question:

1. Can the entire polemic be regarded as a historical encounter between two actual antagonists, rather than as a conventional literary vehicle in which the ostensible literary opponent is merely a fiction mouthing widely known arguments?
2. After all, many of the questions raised by the matrona were regarded as legitimate exegetical problems within the rabbinic schools.

Second the answer:

3. Our proposal that these midrashim be treated as a unit does not depend on a demonstration -- obviously impossible -- that they reflect actual encounters between specific individuals.

Clearly, the authors see a connection between the question and the answer:

1. *Can the entire polemic be regarded....*
2. *After all, many of the questions...*

Then comes:

3. *Our proposal....*

But what, exactly, is the connection between sentences 1 and 2 and sentence 3? I see none at all. The authors win our trust by asking the critical question, how do we know the stories really took place in the second century, involving Yose in particular? But then they make a statement that has no bearing whatsoever on the question. Let me unpack this matter with some care.

First they say that they do not attribute the stories to Yose in particular. Then they talk, rather, about grouping the stories. What connection between the one (1, 2) and the other (3), the question and the answer? The question has not been answered by the answer, because the answer has nothing to do with the question. The answer evades the question, denying its relevance.

But there is the implicit premise, denied by the evasion at hand. I can expose the implicit premise simply by a question of my own: why leap into the second century? It is because, as they explicitly say, "We believe that they record the major arguments in the second century Gnostic-Jewish debate." But why the second century in particular, *if not because Yose is their protagonist?* For if not Yose, then I should think that the third or the fourth centuries offer themselves as candidates.

And, again, if not the second century, then why Gnostic-Jewish debate in particular? Why not a debate within the Jewish community? We could as well interpret the stories as evidence of opinions held within the Jewish community as outside of its borders.

My point should not be lost in a cloud of rhetorical questions. It is very simple. I maintain that Gershenzon and Slomovic fail to answer the question that they ask. To review:

First of all, they deny that the historical question matters. Then, in the very next sentence, they assume the historical question has been settled.

They tell us it does not matter that Yose in particular made these statements. But they tell us that the stories record the major arguments *in the second century Gnostic-Jewish debate as preserved by Jewish spokesmen.*

The upshot may be stated very simply, but requires emphasis:

If it is not the historical Yose in particular, then it is another Jewish spokesman whose name just happened to be Yose.

Failing to read carefully and ask how one sentence logically produces the next, and how a concluding sentence flows logically from the preceding sentences, we are supposed to concede the authors have taken up the critical agenda. They have not even touched it. Let us now reread the concluding paragraph, and see: (1) arguments from content, and (2) the prevailing, but denied, premise that, after all, Yose really said these things, because (3) other things Yose said (not: imputed to Yose) "share distinctive features of style and tone" with these sayings, and, anyhow, (4) in second century Galilee, Gnostics and sages kept meeting, so "almost no other time and place could have been more suitable." So we once more examine *ipsissima verba*:

There are several a priori reasons for treating this group of midrashim as a unit. First, although a wide variety of encounters between sages and matronas is reported in the literature, both in Palestine and in Rome itself, the passages involving R. Jose are unique. They are the only ones which present a straight forward religious polemic in query-answer format. The polemical approach is almost invariably exegetical, a pattern which appears to be characteristic of early refutations of heretical doctrine. All the other passages are anecdotal or episodic, and some have cautionary or legendary overtones. Second, the passages under consideration share distinctive features of style and tone, most notably the homely, almost banal illustrations utilized by R. Jose, and the surprisingly friendly mood of the argument. These features will become apparent upon closer acquaintance. Finally, a brief examination of religious, social and political conditions in second century Galilee suggests that at that time and place an encounter between a leading Jewish sage and an educated Roman aristocrat with Gnostic leanings was, if not routine, quite plausible. Indeed, almost no other time and place could have been more suitable. Let us briefly examine some of these contributing factors.

To conclude:

1. The fact that a number of similar *stories* occur in a number of documents is turned into "a wide variety of *encounters* between sages and matronas is reported in the literature." That is not the fact, only a surmise at best.. The fact is that the similar stories occur a number of times. If we turn that fact into "a wide variety of *encounters*," we are making things up, just as the sages of the Talmud turned two versions of a saying into two stages in Yohanan ben Zakkai's career. The stories may speak of a number of different events. Or they may speak of only one event, told in a number of different ways. Or they may speak of nothing that really happened, but only of something that someone imagines happened.

2. The argument from style is this: the stories share distinctive features of style. But what else does that fact prove? I am baffled. If now the authors do not wish to suggest Yose really said these things, then what historical fact do they hope to demonstrate by showing that fixed and shared literary conventions characterize the genre of story at hand? I imagine they can show a literary fact -- like Cohen, recognizing a convention of genre, but I do not know what *historical* event they therefore allege they have uncovered.

3. The argument from content: this is how we imagine things should have taken place anyhow, so "quite plausible," generates: "no other time and place could have been more suitable." But how do we know unless we compare one proposed context with some other? In fact this is no more than part of the large-scale evasion. I look in vain for any sustained investigation of other times and places. If Gershenzon and Slomovic imagine such possibilities, they do not take them up and show they do not serve, or do not serve so plausibly, as the one at hand.

So to the indictment: the critical agendum makes its appearance, but the authors in the end prove incapable of responding to it at all. They rehearse the argument from content, they appeal to style, they tell us what is plausible -- the usual gullibility. The mark of pseudocritical method I find in the obscurities of a sequence of sentences which, as I read them, have no logical connection from one to the next: gibberish.

To conclude: Gershenzon and Slomovic in their article hardly show the connection between the question:

Can the entire polemic be regarded as a historical encounter

and the answer,

Our proposal...does not depend on a demonstration--obviously impossible--that they reflect actual encounters.

There once again is less here than meets the eye. The evasion consists in three facts.

They evade the historical question (1) by reintroducing what they have just denied:

> *we believe that they record the major arguments in the second century Gnostic Jewish debate, as preserved by Jewish spokesmen.*

So, as I said, it was not the historical Yose, but someone else named Yose (or: many other spokesmen, who as a matter of literary convention all are called Yose?). They evade the historical question (2) by confusing the issue through introducing irrelevant facts of literary convention, treating those facts as if they had a bearing on the historical question, when, in fact, they do not. They evade the historical question (3) by introducing arguments from content: it *sounds* right.

ix

The Future of Gullibility Redivivus

I have raised the issues in work after work for fifteen years. Many, many others have laid out the methodological issues in important articles. But the younger gullible scholars paid no attention. They need not have concurred with my[2] answers, but they did face the responsibility of explaining, in light of my critical program concerning the character and historical usefulness of the texts they cite, why they take for granted if a source assigns a saying to a given rabbi, he really said that saying.

The future works itself out in diverse contexts. Gullibility will flourish as a political force in the ghetto-sector of the Jewish scholarly world. It has no future at all outside of the institutions of that world, since, without the walls of ghettos to protect it, the scholarly equivalent of belief that the world is flat and that the sun goes around the earth cannot sustain itself. Gullibility invokes its own self-evidence. Where people find self-evident the convictions and propositions of scholarly gullibility, they will write articles and even books like those we have examined. Where people find self-evident the methods and principles of critical learning in the Western humanities, they will write articles and books like mine -- or, I hope, better ones: more abstract, more

---

[2]In fact "my" program simply recapitulates in the present context the established critical program of Western academic learning.

encompassing, more venturesome and imaginative.   That is the future: two worlds, each in its orbit, never to meet, except to collide.

It remains to ask, what price gullibility? The cost to the study of the texts at hand -- which the believers claim to prize -- is incalculable. For the believers insist on asking questions the holy books do not answer, and they also do not wish to listen to the answers the holy books give to questions the holy books do take up. So the Orthodox, the religious fundamentalists, the credulous and the believers whatever their belief, -- above all the gullible scholars reject what the sources at hand wish to teach and impose a program of inquiries about what someone "really said or did on that day," for which the sources scarcely serve. We cannot ask religious texts that by no reasonable standard can tell us what really happened on a given day long before the texts' own redaction to report to us about "that day." Nor can we demand that that authorship record what Yose really thought, or about how "the rabbis" said this or did that or changed their policy in such and such a way. Texts written down centuries beyond the point purportedly under discussion cannot have much information on those matters. We can and should ask the texts to give us their messages and to convey their meanings. But the believers do not want to listen to those messages, and that is a loss -- to the holy books. For the true believers do not want to pay attention to the convictions important to the authorship of the holy books. The victim of the sin of gullibility is the canon that the believers claim to hold dear. They want what the sources do not give, and they do not want what the sources provide in abundance. And that is the principal cost. Now to consider the alternative: why this, not that.

Part Four

THE WAY FORWARD

Chapter Five

Parsing the Rabbinic Canon

Having shown that what others attempt to do rests on a false premise as to the character of the evidence, let me now explain the alternative. The canonical writings under study constitute not sources for historical study but documents of a religious culture. Therefore we should ask questions of a religious rather than of a historical character. The evidence testifies to a religious system, and it should be read for the study of the character of a religious system: the description, analysis, and interpretation of the Judaism written down in these books. To state my premise simply: religions constitute systems, systems of culture. Documents of religions express in detail the larger system of which they form a part, the detail containing within itself the structure of the whole. What demands description therefore are categories defined not by names of authorities, let alone by rubrics of dogmatic theology, but by the artifacts of a cultural system, in the case of rabbinic writings, the documents themselves. We miss the point of the sources when we ask the sources to tell us what really happened, that is to say, when we frame our questions, not theirs. The authorships whose works we study wished to make points of their own. To begin with, we have to learn to listen to those points -- their matters of emphasis, not ours. Otherwise we fail to attend to what the sources wish to tell us, choosing rather to listen to ourselves and our own messages.

Insisting on the "historicity" of attributions, which characterizes the bulk of work done these days as in times past, leads to asking the wrong questions, namely, questions of historical fact. More consequentially, that same attitude of mind obscures the right questions, specifically, questions of cultural order, social system and political structure, to which the texts respond explicitly and constantly. Confronting writings of a religious character, we err by asking questions of a narrowly historical character: what did X really say -- or think! -- on a particular occasion, and why. These questions not only are not answerable on the basis of the evidence in hand. They also are trivial, irrelevant to the character of the evidence. What strikes me as I review the writings just now cited is how little of real interest and worth we should know, even if we were to concede the historical accuracy and veracity of all the many allegations of the scholars we have surveyed. How little we should know -- but how much we should have *missed* if that set of questions and answers were to encompass the whole of our inquiry.

Religious systems, after all, concern the on-going and enduring rules of a holy community, and the one thing that a religious document does not consider interesting on a routine basis is the particular and the one-time event. The givens that govern all events -- God's will and rule for reality -- find exemplification in the religious record of the one-time and the particular. For when religions do speak of the unique and the particular, they lead us to the center and heart of their systems. They therefore do not regard the everyday happening as unique and worthy of historical note on its own. The contrast to the fundamental conviction of historical writing should not be missed. When histories take up the unique, they address the one-time and specific and everyday. But when religions consider the unique. they address -- and reveal -- what is at the center of their systems. These simply are not the same thing. When religious writings, therefore, tell us what happened, it is to exemplify a rule -- and the rule is what counts. So when we turn to essentially religious texts and believe everything they tell us about things that happened, we do not hear what those documents actually record and report. It is not the event -- which is essentially beside the point -- but the rule exemplified by the event.

In the rabbinic canon we deal with documents of a religious system, statements of a world view and prescription of a way of life meant to define a social world, a *Judaism* of an *Israel*. To ask those documents to report, like daily newspapers, on events of a routine, adventitious character, is to misunderstand their purpose and character. To invoke their power to describe a social world, to lead us into the details of a cogent cultural system -- that is to learn what the documents, as a matter of fact, record accurately, copiously, authoritatively. And yet at issue is not simply the right questions and the wrong ones. It is to begin with the simpler issue of gullibility, framed throughout the preceding chapters. Let me explain the right way of viewing things, having proved beyond doubt the prevalence of the wrong one.

When studying topics in the Judaism of the sages of the rabbinic writings from the first through the seventh centuries, as we have seen, people routinely cite sayings categorized by attribution rather than document. That is to say, they treat as one group of sayings whatever is assigned to Rabbi X. This is without regard to the documents in which those sayings occur, where or when those documents reached closure, and similar considerations of literary context and documentary circumstance. The category defined by attributions to a given authority rests on the premise that the things given in the name of Rabbi X really were said by him. No other premise would justify resort to the category deriving from use of a name, that alone. Commonly, the next step is to treat those sayings as evidence of ideas held, if not by that particular person, then by people in the age in which the cited authority lived. Once more the premise that the sayings go back to the age, if not the person, of the authority to whom they are attributed underpins further inquiry. Accordingly, scholars cite sayings in the name of given authorities and take for granted that those sayings were said by the authority to whom they were attributed and, of course, in the time in which that authority flourished.

By contrast, I treat the historical sequence of sayings only in accord with the order of the documents in which they first occur. Let me expand on why I have taken the approach that I have. Since many sayings are attributed to specific authorities, why not lay out the sayings in the order of the authorities to whom they are attributed, rather than in the order of the books in which these sayings occur? It is because the attributions cannot be validated, but the books can.

The system of Judaism attested by the canon at hand reached its first literary expression in ca. 200 C.E. and its last in ca. 600 C.E. The first document, the Mishnah, drew together teachings of authorities of the period beginning in the first century, before 70, when the Temple was destroyed and autonomous government ended, and ending with the publication of the code in ca. 200. The last, the Talmud of Babylonia (Bavli) provided the authoritative commentary on thirty-seven of the sixty-two tractates of the Mishnah as well as on substantial portions of the Hebrew Scriptures. In joining sustained discourse on the Scriptures, called, in the mythic of the present system, the Written Torah, as well as on the Mishnah, held to be the Oral, or memorized Torah, the Bavli's framers presented a summa, an encyclopaedia, of Judaism, to guide Israel, the Jewish people, for many centuries to come.

In-between ca. 200, when autonomous government was well established again, and ca. 600 the continuous and ongoing movement of sages, holding positions of authority in the Jewish governments recognized by Rome and Iran, as political leaders of the Jewish communities of the Land of Israel (to just after 400 C.E.) and Babylonia (to about 500 C.E.), respectively, wrote two types of books. One sort extended, amplified, systematized, and harmonized components of the legal system laid forth in the Mishnah. The work of Mishnah-exegesis produced four principal documents as well as an apologia for the Mishnah.

This last -- the rationale or apologia -- came first in time, about a generation or so beyond the publication of the Mishnah itself. It was tractate Abot, ca. 250 C.E., a collection of sayings attributed both to authorities whose names occur, also, in the Mishnah, as well as to some sages who flourished after the conclusion of the Mishnah. These later figures, who make no appearance in that document, stand at the end of the compilation. The other three continuators of the Mishnah were the Tosefta, the Talmud of the Land of Israel (the Yerushalmi), and the Bavli. The Tosefta, containing a small proposition of materials contemporaneous with those presently in the Mishnah and a very sizable proportion secondary to, and dependent, even verbatim, on the Mishnah, reached conclusion some time after ca. 300 and before ca. 400. The Yerushalmi closed at ca. 400. The Bavli, as I said, was completed by ca. 600. All these dates, of course, are rough guesses, but the sequence in which the documents made their appearance is not.

The Tosefta addresses the Mishnah; its name means "supplement," and its function was to supplement the rules of the original documents. The Yerushalmi mediates between the Tosefta and the Mishnah, commonly citing a paragraph of the Tosefta in juxtaposition with a paragraph of the Mishnah and commenting on both, or so arranging matters that the paragraph of the Tosefta serves, just as it should, to complement a paragraph of the Mishnah. The Bavli, following the Yerushalmi by about two centuries, pursues its own program, which, as I said, was to link the two Torahs and restate them as one.

The stream of exegesis of the Mishnah and exploration of its themes of law and philosophy flowed side by side with a second. This other river coursed up out of the deep wells of the written Scripture. But it surfaced only long after the work of Mishnah-exegesis was well underway and followed the course of that exegesis, now extended to Scripture. The exegesis of the Hebrew Scriptures, a convention of all systems of Judaism from before the conclusion of Scripture itself, obviously occupied sages from the very origins of their group. No one began anywhere but in the encounter with the Written Torah. But the writing down of exegeses of Scripture in a systematic way, signifying also the formulation of a program and a plan for the utilization of the Written Torah in the unfolding literature of the Judaism taking shape in the centuries at hand, developed in a quite distinct circumstance.

Specifically, one fundamental aspect of the work of Mishnah-exegesis began with one ineluctable question. How does a rule of the Mishnah relate to, or rest upon, a rule of Scripture? That question demanded an answer, so that the status of the Mishnah's rules, and, right alongside, of the Mishnah itself, could find a clear definition. Standing by itself, the Mishnah bore no explanation of why Israel should obey its rules and accept its vision. Brought into relationship to Scriptures, in mythic language, viewed as part of the Torah, the Mishnah gained access to the source of authority by definition operative in Israel, the Jewish people. Accordingly, the work of relating the Mishnah's rules to those of Scripture got under way alongside the formation of the Mishnah's rules themselves. Collecting and arranging exegeses of Scripture as these related to passages of the Mishnah first reached literary form in the Sifra, to Leviticus, and in two books, both called Sifré, one to Numbers, the other Deuteronomy. All three compositions accomplished much else. For, even at that early stage, exegeses of passages of Scripture in their own context and not only for the sake of Mishnah-exegesis attracted attention. But a principal motif in all three books concerned the issue of Mishnah-Scripture relationships.

A second, still more fruitful path also emerged from the labor of Mishnah-exegesis. As the work of Mishnah-exegesis got under way, in the third century, exegetes of the Mishnah and others alongside undertook a parallel labor. It was to work through verses of Scripture in exactly the same way -- word for word, phrase for phrase, line for line -- in which, to begin with, the exegetes of the Mishnah pursued the interpretation and explanation of the Mishnah. To state matters simply, precisely the types of exegesis that dictated the way in which sages read the Mishnah now guided their reading of Scripture as well. And, as people began to collect and organize comments in accord with the order of sentences and paragraphs of the Mishnah, they found the stimulation to collect and organize comments on clauses and verses of Scripture. As I said, this kind of work got under way in the Sifra and the two Sifrés. It reached massive and magnificent fulfillment in Genesis Rabbah, which, as its name tells us, presents a line-for-line reading of the book of Genesis.

Beyond these two modes of exegesis and the organization of exegesis in books, first on the Mishnah, then on Scripture, lies yet a third. To understand it, we once more turn back to the Mishnah's great exegetes, represented to begin with in the Yerushalmi. While the original exegesis of the Mishnah in the Tosefta addressed the document under study through a line by line commentary, responding only in discrete and self-contained units of discourse, authors of units of discourse gathered in the next, the Yerushalmi, developed yet another mode of discourse entirely. They treated not phrases or sentences but principles and large-scale conceptual problems. They dealt not alone with a given topic, a subject and its rule, but with an encompassing problem, a principle and its implications for a number of topics and rules. This far more discursive and philosophical mode of thought produced for Mishnah-exegesis, in somewhat smaller volume but in much richer contents, sustained essays on principles cutting across specific rules. And for Scripture the work of sustained and broad-ranging discourse resulted in a second type of exegetical work, beyond that focused on words, phrases, and sentences.

Discursive exegesis is represented, to begin with, in Leviticus Rabbah, a document that reached closure, people generally suppose, sometime after Genesis Rabbah, thus in ca. 400-500, one might guess. Leviticus Rabbah presents not phrase-by-phrase systematic exegeses of verses in the book of Leviticus, but a set of thirty-seven topical essays. These essays, syllogistic in purpose, take the form of citations and comments on verses of Scripture to be sure. But the compositions range widely over the far reaches of the Hebrew Scriptures while focusing narrowly upon a given theme. They moreover make quite distinctive points about that theme. Their essays constitute compositions, not merely composites. Whether devoted to God's favor to the poor and humble or to the dangers of drunkenness, the essays, exegetical in form, discursive in character, correspond to the equivalent, legal essays, amply represented in the Yerushalmi.

So in this other mode of Scripture-interpretation, too, the framers of the exegeses of Scripture accomplished in connection with Scripture what the Yerushalmi's exegetes of the Mishnah were doing in the same way at the same time. We move rapidly past yet a third mode of Scriptural exegesis, one in which the order of Scripture's verses is left far behind, and in which topics, not passages of Scripture, take over as the mode of organizing thought. Represented by Pesiqta deR. Kahana, Lamentations Rabbati, and some other collections conventionally assigned to the sixth and seventh centuries, these entirely discursive compositions move out in their own direction, only marginally relating in mode of discourse to any counterpart types of composition in the Yerushalmi (or in the Bavli).

At the end of the extraordinary creative age of Judaism, the authors of units of discourse collected in the Bavli drew together the two, up-to-then distinct, modes of organizing thought, either around the Mishnah or around Scripture. They treated both Torahs, oral and written, as equally available in the work of organizing large-scale exercises of sustained inquiry. So we find in the Bavli a systematic treatment of some tractates of the Mishnah. And within the same aggregates of discourse, we also find (in somewhat smaller proportion to be sure, roughly 60% to roughly 40% in the sample I made of three tractates) a second principle of organizing and redaction. That principle dictates that ideas be laid out in line with verses of Scripture, themselves dealt with in cogent sequence, one by one, just as the Mishnah's sentences and paragraphs come under analysis, in cogent order and one by one.

The reason that the foregoing, somewhat protracted theory of the development and organization of the sources of formative Judaism requires attention is simple. If we are to trace the unfolding, in the sources of formative Judaism, of a given theme or ideas on a given problem, the order in which we approach the several books, that is, components of the entire canon, gives us the sole guidance on sequence, order, and context, that we are apt to find. How so? We have no way of demonstrating that authorities to whom, in a given composition, ideas are attributed really said what is assigned to them. The sole fact in hand therefore is that the framers of a given document included in their book sayings imputed to named authorities. Are these dependable? Unlikely on the face of it. Why not? Since the same sayings will be imputed to diverse authorities by different groups of editors, of different books, we stand on shaky ground indeed if we rely for chronology upon the framers' claims of who said what. More important, attributions by themselves cannot be shown to be reliable. *What we cannot show we do not know.* Lacking firm evidence, for example, in a sage's own, clearly assigned writings, or even in writings redacted by a sage's own disciples and handed on among them in the discipline of their own community, we have for chronology only a single fact.

It is that a document, reaching closure at a given time, contains the allegation that Rabbi X said statement Y. So we know that people at the time of the document reached closure took the view that Rabbi X said statement Y. We may then assign to statement Y a position, in the order of the sequence of sayings, defined by the location of the document in the order of the sequence of documents. The several documents' dates, as is clear, all constitute guesses. But the sequence Mishnah, Tosefta, Yerushalmi, Bavli for the exegetical writings on the Mishnah is absolutely firm and beyond doubt. The sequence for the exegetical collections on Scripture Sifra, the Sifrés, Genesis Rabbah, Leviticus

Rabbah, the Pesiqtas and beyond is not entirely sure. Still the position of the Sifra and the two Sifrés at the head, followed by Genesis Rabbah, then Leviticus Rabbah, then Pesiqta deR. Kahana and Lamentations Rabbati and some related collections, seems likely.

What then constitutes the history of an idea in formative Judaism? We trace what references we find to a topic in accord with the order of documents just now spelled out. In this sort of study we learn the order in which ideas came to expression in the canon. We begin any survey with the Mishnah, the starting point of the canon. We proceed systematically to work our way through tractate Abot, the Mishnah's first apologetic, then the Tosefta, the Yerushalmi, and the Bavli at the end. In a single encompassing sweep, we finally deal with the entirety of the compilations of the exegeses of Scripture, arranged, to be sure, in that order that I have now explained.

Let me expand on the matter of my heavy emphasis on the order of the components of the canon. The reason for that stress is simple. We have to ask not only what documents viewed whole and all at once ("Judaism") tell us about our theme. In tracing the order in which ideas make their appearance, we ask about the components in sequence ("history of Judaism") so far as we can trace the sequence. Then and only then shall we have access to issues of *history*, that is, of change and development. If our theme makes its appearance early on in one form, so one set of ideas predominate in a document that reached closure in the beginnings of the cannon and then that theme drops out of public discourse or undergoes radical revision in writings in later stages of the canon, that fact may make considerable difference. Specifically, we may find it possible to speculate on where, and why a given approach proved urgent, and also on the reasons that that same approach receded from the center of interest.

To conclude: since the various compositions of the canon of formative Judaism derive not from named, individual authors but from collective decisions of schools or academies, we cannot take for granted attributions of sayings to individuals provide facts. We cannot show that if a given rabbi is alleged to have made a statement, he really did say what is assigned to him. We do not have a book or a letter he wrote such as we have, for example, for Paul or Augustine or other important Christian counterparts to the great rabbis of late antiquity. We also do not know that if a story was told, things really happened in the way the story-teller says, in some other way, or not at all. Accordingly, we cannot identify as historical in a narrow and exact sense anything that comes down to us in the canon of Judaism. What is absolutely firm and factual, by contrast, is that these books represent views held by the authorship behind them. At the point at which a document reached conclusion and redaction, views of a given group of people reached the form at that moment of closure in which we now have them (taking account of for variations of wording). That is why I do not allege we know what people were thinking prior to the point at which, it is generally assumed, a given document was redacted. Accordingly, if I wish to know the sequence in which views reached their current expression, I have recourse to the conventional order and rough dating assigned by modern scholarship to the several documents, from the Mishnah through the Bavli.

Still more critical, in knowing the approximate sequence of documents and therefore the ideas in them (at least so far as the final point at which those ideas reached formal expression in the canon), a second possibility emerges. What if -- as is the case -- we find pretty much the same views, treated in the same proportion and for the same purpose, yielding the same message, early, middle, and late in the development of the canon? Then we shall have to ask why the literature remains so remarkably constant. Given the considerable shifts in the social and political condition of Israel in the land of Israel as well as in Babylonia over a period of more than four hundred years, that evident stability in the teachings for the affective life will constitute a considerable fact for analysis and interpretation.

History done rightly thus produces two possibilities, both of them demanding sustained attention. Things change. Why? Things do not change. Why not? We may well trace the relationship between the history of ideas and the history of the society that holds those same ideas. We follow the interplay between society and system -- world view, way of life, addressed to a particular social group -- by developing a theory of the relationship between contents and context, between the world in which people live and the world which people create in their shared social and imaginative life. When we can frame a theory of how a system in substance relates to its setting, of the interplay between the social matrix and the mode and manner of a society's world-view and way of life, then we may develop theses of general intelligibility, theories of why this, not that, of why, and why not and how come. And that I conceive to be the purpose of academic learning in a free society and in a free academy.

Index

BROWN JUDAIC STUDIES SERIES

Continued from back cover